How to Manage an
Effective
Religious
Organization

How to Manage an
EFFECTIVE
RELIGIOUS
ORGANIZATION

The Essential Guide to Improving Your Church,
Synagogue, Mosque, or Temple

By Michael A. Sand

CAREER
PRESS

Pompton Plains, NJ

HOW TO MANAGE AN EFFECTIVE RELIGIOUS ORGANIZATION
EDITED AND TYPESET BY DIANA GHAZZAWI
Cover design by Dutton and Sherman Design
Printed in the U.S.A.

To order this title, please call toll-free 1-800-CAREER-1 (NJ and Canada: 201-848-0310) to order using VISA or MasterCard, or for fur-ther information on books from Career Press.

The Career Press, Inc.
220 West Parkway, Unit 12
Pompton Plains, NJ 07444
www.careerpress.com

Library of Congress Cataloging-in-Publication Data
Sand, Michael A.
    How to manage an effective religious organization : the essential guide to improving your church, synagogue, mosque, or temple / by Michael A. Sand
        p. cm.
    Includes bibliographical references and index.
    ISBN 978-1-60163-151-0 -- ISBN 978-1-60163-675-1 (ebook)
        1. Management--Religious aspects. I. Title.

HD31.S316 2011
206--dc22

2011003525

This book is dedicated to the memory of Sandra Eckert. Though she lost her battle with cancer, she left a legacy of love, dignity, and caring.

Acknowledgments

It takes a village to write a book that will be helpful to millions of individuals who are members of many different religions. Special thanks to my research assistant, Barbara Trainin Blank; my wife, Diane Z. Sand; and my agent, Sara Camilli. I appreciated the help of Rev. Dick Dowhower, Rev. Sandra Strauss, Rev. LaVette Paige, Deacon Charles Clark, Fr. Jim Podlesny, Diana Robertson, and many other religious and lay leaders.

Contents

Introduction

There are more than one million nonprofit organizations in the United States. How many you can name that affect your life? Yes, the museum you attended on your vacation is nonprofit, the hospital where your child was born may be, and the homeless shelter you contributed to definitely is.

But how about a nonprofit that you may attend every week and whose decisions affected you when you were born and married, and will affect your family when you die? Surely, we are talking about your place of worship, whether you call it a church, synagogue, temple, mosque, or some other name. There are more nonprofits in the United States that are houses of worship than any other type of nonprofits. How many houses of worship are there in the United States? How many individuals attend these houses of worship?

The most accurate answer is we do not know for sure. Because of court interpretations of the First Amendment to the United States Constitution, the government does not require religious institutions to register. Therefore, you can form a new religion without listing it anywhere, and no one knows for sure how many individuals attend religious services. The Hartford Institute for Religion Research estimates there are 335,000 religious congregations in the United States. The vast majority of these congregations, or 322,000, are Christian.[1] And Americans worship regularly: the Gallup Research Organization estimates 40 percent of all Americans, or roughly 118 million individuals, attended worship services the previous weekend.[2]

We do know that the United States is a very religious country. ProCon.org states there are 313 different religions in the United States.[3] Of the 196,319,700 Americans older than the age of 18, a total of 166,887,700 or 85 percent state they belong to one of these religious groups.[4]

The Pew Forum on Religion & Public Life confirms that the United States is a predominantly Christian country. It reports that 78.4 percent of adults in the United States are Christian; only 4.7 percent are adherents of other religions. The Pew study reports that the remaining 16.1 percent of Americans are "Unaffiliated."[5]

Your Religious Organization

What do you know about the religious organization where you spend the most time? The church, synagogue, mosque, or temple affects your life when you are born, attend educational programs, attend daily or weekly religious services, attend special services on religious holidays, get married, and die. If you are among the nearly 83 percent of Americans who identify themselves as belonging to a religious faith, you have all these connections. Yet, what do you know about how your religious organization is run?

- When you put funds in the collection plate, pay dues, or contribute to a stewardship campaign, what happens to these funds?
- What is the church's budget?
- Who makes decisions about temple expenditures?
- Can your mosque receive faith-based grants?
- Did anyone ever ask you for suggestions about how you can help your church or how your church can help you?
- If you have a complaint, how do you raise it?
- How was the minister hired?
- How can you have input into the evaluation of the minister?
- Who sits on the church council?
- What are the responsibilities of the church council?
- How can your synagogue recruit more effective volunteers?

If you want to know the answers to any of these questions, this book is for *you*. It will give you information about the ways religious institutions can improve their management. It will suggest questions to ask about the management of your congregation and whom you should ask these questions.

One thing is clear from the outset: every single religious organization has the same basic challenges. By reading this book, you will get some tips for increasing the number and quality of volunteers, improving governance, getting and keeping new members, and raising funds, no matter what your religious affiliation. This book will not provide *all* the answers, but it will provide *some* answers and will suggest numerous questions you should be asking if you want to improve your religious institution.

Terminology

One of the initial difficulties in writing this book is the terminology. Some individuals call their place of worship a *church*, others a *synagogue*, a *mosque*, a *temple*, and numerous other names. This book talks about principles that would be helpful in each of these houses of worship. So I had to make an arbitrary decision. Because most individuals in the United States refer to their place of worship as a church, I will use that term to refer to all places of worship.

What about the religious leader? Again, there is wide divergence in terminology. Some refer to the religious leader as *imam*; others use the term *minister, priest, pastor, rabbi,* or *reverend*. Again I had to make an arbitrary decision. Because most Americans (51.3 percent) identify themselves as Protestant, I will use Protestant terminology. Thesaurus.com states "a minister is commonly a person who leads the congregation of a Protestant church."[6] For this reason, throughout this book the religious leader is referred to as the *minister*.

How about the group of lay leaders that sets or recommends policy? Some religious institutions call it the *board*, the *council*, the *governing board*, the *board of trustees*, the *pastoral council*, or a host of different names. I will use the term *council* to refer to this body.

To make things more complicated, the head of the council is called by different names. In some groups, it is the *president*, in others the *chair*, the *chairman*, the *chairperson*, and many other terms. For the sake of consistency, I will refer to the chief elected officer as the *chair*.

So if I talk about the minister having a discussion with the church council, if you are Jewish, you know I am referring to the rabbi having a discussion with the synagogue board; if you are Muslim, the imam is meeting with the board at the mosque.

If matters were not complicated enough, numerous religious organizations have a body to which they belong. The duties of this body differ widely and are discussed throughout this book. The names of these bodies differ widely as well. Here are but a few of the names:

Presbyterian Church	➤	Presbytery
Lutheran Church	➤	Synod
Conservative Synagogue	➤	United Synagogue of Conservative Judaism
Baha'i Faith	➤	Universal House of Justice
United Church of Christ	➤	General Synod
Methodist Church	➤	General Conference
Quaker	➤	General Conference of the Religious Society of Friends

Because these umbrella bodies have so many different names and responsibilities, I will refer to them as *judicatories* throughout this book.

Book Sections

You can use this book in any way that is convenient. Some may read it cover to cover. Others may use it as a reference book and read individual chapters when a need arises. Chapters 1–4 are on hiring, helping, evaluating, and firing the religious leader. Chapters 5–8 deal with leading the religious organization, offering information on the council, meaningful by-laws, forming active committees, and personnel policies.

Financial matters are discussed in Chapters 9–12, with chapters on fundraising, fiscal procedures and cutting expenditures, capital campaigns, and faith-based grant writing. Chapters 13–16 are about making members happy and filling the pews, and include information on strategic planning, membership and programs, getting and keeping volunteers, and meaningful life-cycle events. Chapter 17 concludes with a checklist for every individual sitting in the pews, serving on the council, or employed as church staff to determine if you have an excellent religious institution.

1

Hiring the Religious Leader

The most important decision religious organizations make is the hiring of the religious leader. All members of the congregation should be informed of the process used to hire this leader, whether priest, minister, rabbi, or imam. It is important that these procedures be established in writing before any search begins. The congregants should be notified of these procedures. Often they are published in the parish bulletin.

As a congregant, learn the steps for hiring in your particular religious organization, because these steps differ widely. Find out the opportunities for input so you can include your recommendations in this important decision. There are numerous models for acquiring a religious leader and many variations among the models. Here are four main models:

- Congregation is assigned religious leader.
- Congregation hires religious leader.
- Volunteer religious leader is selected.
- Some faiths do not have religious leaders.

Congregation Is Assigned Religious Leader

The priest for each Catholic church is assigned by the bishop.[1] If a parish priest position is open, priests in the area are notified of the vacancy in case they would like to be appointed to the position. The bishop tries to place the priest with the appropriate congregation. A priest can say he does not think a certain place is good for him.

A congregation with a priest vacancy might make its needs known to the bishop. For example, a congregation may request a younger priest because it has young parishioners with many children. It may request an older priest because many of its members are senior citizens.

In some Protestant faiths, the minister is assigned a congregation. The United Methodist Church concept of "pastoral charge" includes the bishop appointing the church pastors and holding them responsible for what happens in the church.[2]

Congregation Hires Religious Leader

It is common for a congregation to hire and pay its own religious leader. The variations on the procedures to meet the goal of selecting the most qualified candidate are extensive.

Islam is an example of a religion in which the congregation, as represented by the council, hires its religious leader, the imam. The document "Hiring an Imam" (madisonmuslims.org) included as Appendix 1, was prepared by the Masjid Us Sunnah, a mosque in Madison, Wisconsin, and can be used as a model for other faiths hiring their religious leaders.

This document indicates "The Imam Hiring Committee (IHC) is assigned the task of searching for and selecting an imam for the community." The tasks of the hiring committee are spelled out and can be helpful to any religious organization:

1. Adhere to strict confidentiality at all steps of the process.
2. Define community needs. Ask people for input.
3. Conduct a feasibility study to determine if the community can afford an imam.
4. List desired qualifications of imam. Ask people for input.
5. List imam's duties. Ask people for input.
6. Develop interview questions. Ask qualified people.
7. Develop evaluation criteria.
8. Solicit candidates.
9. Screen candidates.
10. Interview candidates.
11. Document candidate questions and requirements.
12. Check references and background of finalist(s).
13. Make recommendations of finalist(s) to the Board.[3]

All congregations hiring their religious leaders follow a variation of this hiring process.

Selection of the Search Committee

Although most religious organizations select a search committee to interview prospective religious leader candidates, the process differs widely. In the Jewish and Unitarian Universalist faiths, the chairman of the board appoints the members of the search committee. In the Baptist faith, the congregation selects the members.

The Presbyterian Church (USA), in the "Committee on Ministry Advisory Handbook," spells out the procedures clearly. These procedures can be used by other faith communities. First, the Pastor Nominating Committee (PNC) is elected by the congregation as a whole and reports to the congregation regularly. The church calls a congregational meeting for the purpose of electing the PNC, providing for the appropriate amount of time for public notice (on two successive Sundays). At the congregational meeting, nominations from the floor are also in order. The PNC should not only be representative of the congregation in terms of age, gender, ethnic background, and involvement within the church, but also should include active church members who:

- Have a deep and abiding faith.
- Are secure and independent thinkers.
- Can make this responsibility a high priority.
- Can be trusted with confidential information.
- Are good listeners who work well with others.
- Have a dedication to the Presbyterian search process.
- Trust in the movement of God's Spirit as part of that process.[4]

The *United Church of Christ Search and Call Process* lists the qualifications of the search committee members as follows:

There are a number of personal qualities and attributes to consider in the selection of search committee members; individuals should have:

- A passionate commitment to Christ's church.
- A positive attitude (no grudges!).

- A capacity to approach the task with openness rather than a pre-determined agenda.
- A sense of integrity and respect for others.
- An ability to be absolutely confidential.
- A capacity to listen, to participate in a group, and to come to consensus.

In addition, an individual under consideration for the search committee should be:

- An active supporter of the church as demonstrated by worship attendance, financial support, and participation.
- Trusted and respected by the congregation.
- Willing and able to make this responsibility a very high priority.[5]

The United Church of Christ bulletin gives the following specific advice on the composition of the search committee:

> The experience of other churches would suggest that the Search Committee be composed of five to nine members with the president/moderator a non-voting member. Two persons from the same family should not be asked to serve. As much as possible, the committee should be selected to include an equal representation of men and women, young and old, new and long-time members, as well as persons with involvement in varied aspects of church life (choir, educational ministry, women's or men's groups, deacons, mission and outreach). The members should reflect, as much as possible, the diversity of the congregation (racial, cultural, economic, sexual orientation) and there should be at least one youth member.[6]

John Vonhof, in The Alban Guide for Managing the Pastoral Search Process, states "it is crucial for the search committee to be made up of a cross section of the membership of the congregation." He recommends that committee members rank high in four areas— spiritual sensitivity, ability to work well in a committee setting, listening and communication skills, and ability to take an active role in the ministries of the church.[7]

These are the duties of the search committee:

- Develop job description.
- Obtain lists of candidates.
- Screen candidates.
- Interview candidates.
- Check references.
- Recommend religious leader.

Selecting Candidates to Interview

Here, too, there are numerous variations when selecting candidates to interview. Some congregations make up a help-wanted ad and put it in the local newspaper and the church bulletin. They also send the ad to a state, regional, or national religious body for publication. In many faiths, a national body collects information from individuals who wish to serve as religious leaders for congregations. This is an important service, as the national body will certify that the candidate has the appropriate ordination in that religion.

Religious groups differ widely as to which candidates the local religious organization can interview. For example, Appendix 2 is a newspaper advertisement for an imam placed by the Islamic Society in Alabama.

The manual for the United Church of Christ has another approach. It directs each local church to look for candidates on the UCC Website and actively discourages seeking candidates in any other way:

> Publicizing your pastoral position on the UCC Website is an essential step in the Search and Call process. However, it is NOT desirable to attempt to seek candidates by advertising on the Internet, in newspapers, or in other 'public' settings. It is not in your church's best interests to open yourselves to unsolicited applications from candidates about whom you will have difficulty obtaining honest and reliable information. You have a covenantal responsibility to provide the safest possible environment for the children, youth, and adults who participate in your church. By remaining within the UCC Search and Call system, you can be assured that both

an employment history and a criminal background check have been carried out for each candidate whose Ministerial Profile you receive. Your committee is also urged to use discretion in terms of the information about the search process that is included in your own church's web site. Posting updates for your members may be helpful, but you should emphasize that you are not open to unsolicited applications because you are receiving all Ministerial Profiles through your Conference/Association office.[8]

Jewish congregations in the Conservative branch are forbidden to recruit rabbinical candidates and may only interview candidates whose resumes are sent to them by their national organization, the Rabbinical Assembly.[9]

Initial Screening and Telephone Interviews

Many search committees establish a small subcommittee to review the resumes that have been submitted and decide which candidates should be interviewed by telephone. Some committees have just one member conduct phone interviews; others schedule conference calls with several members present or set up a speakerphone interview. Make certain to ask all candidates the same questions. Each candidate should be asked for permission to have the initial interview by telephone. It is appropriate to ask candidates to send you at least one audio or video sermon before conducting the phone interview.

Selecting Candidates for In-Person Interviews

The next step is to recommend to the search committee which candidates should be invited to meet for in-person interviews. Again, practices differ widely. Some search committees invite only the candidate they feel from the telephone interview will be the most qualified candidate. Others may invite several candidates for in-person interviews.

Checking References

Check references supplied by all candidates who are being invited for a personal interview. The manual of the Presbyterian Church (USA) *On Calling a Pastor* includes excellent tips for checking references of pastoral candidates. On the application form the candidate fills out, he/she is required to give up to six references. The publication recommends that a member of the search committee call each reference by phone and ask the same list of prepared questions to each reference.

In order to help ensure the information is reliable, ask the reference to respond only on the basis of firsthand knowledge, rather than rumors or impressions that cannot be substantiated. When negative references are received, they should be carefully checked.

Begin the telephone call by describing your congregation and community and then ask the reference to give an assessment of how the prospective pastor might serve in your setting. It is appropriate to ask questions such as "How does Pastor X deal with conflict?" Ask questions that focus on the ability of the candidate to be an effective minister. The manual recommends that the final question be "Is there anything else we should know?"

The Presbyterian document states that under no circumstances should a search committee member contact members of a prospective pastor's present congregation without his or her permission to do so.[10]

John Vonhof, in The Alban Guide to Managing the Pastoral Search Process, suggests asking the following sample questions:

- How long have you known Pastor _____?
- What ministry relationships have you had with Pastor _____?
- Can you state Pastor _____'s vision?
- How does Pastor _____ lead his/her congregation?
- How does Pastor _____ develop personal growth in his/her ministry?
- How does Pastor _____ challenge the congregation?
- Please describe what area of Pastor _____'s ministry is his/her greatest strength and ability.
- Are there any areas of Pastor's ministry that could benefit from development and attention?
- How do you feel about Pastor _____'s credibility?
- Do you have any other candid and confidential comments you would like to share?[11]

The United Church of Christ recommends that each reference be sent a written request for information about a potential candidate. A detailed questionnaire for the reference to fill out is included in Appendix 3.

Church Profile and Pastoral Questionnaire

One important factor in hiring a religious leader is providing candidates with a profile of your religious organization and community. The congregation wants to hire a religious leader who "fits." One way to help ensure this is to spell out as much information as possible about the congregation and community. An excellent questionnaire for the church to fill out is provided by the United Church of Christ. It can be found at *www.ucc.org/ministers/pdfs/local-church-profile-pdf-revised-7-07.pdf*. It is strongly recommended that every religious organization fill out a questionnaire and provide it to every candidate.

John Vonhof, in The Alban Guide to Managing the Pastoral Search Process, suggests each prospective minister be sent a videotape. It might include children and youth programs, choir practices, Sunday school classes and the church grounds, facilities, and parsonage.[12] Another excellent suggestion is to ask the candidates to provide information about themselves before the interview. A sample Pastoral Questionnaire is provided in Appendix 4.

Interviewing Candidates

All candidates likely to be hired should be invited for a personal interview. Hiring committees differ on who does the interviewing. In many religious organizations, the president of the church council and the chair of the hiring committee interview all candidates.

Some groups include a few additional interviewers; often, the entire search committee does the interviewing. The committee should meet before the interview so all members can review the resume of the candidate and be told about information obtained from the telephone interview and the reference checks. A list of questions should be developed that will be asked of all interviewees. One individual should be designated to ask most of the questions.

The United Church of Christ's Search and Call Process offers several recommendations for the interview process:

- Review the candidate's profile prior to the interview.
- Review your church's Local Church Profile.
- Wear name tags.
- Plan the interview questions carefully.
- One person, usually the chair, should manage the flow of the interview.
- Pray together.
- Plan for no more than one and a half hours.
- Leave ample time for the candidate's questions of your committee.
- Listen.
- Ask questions for clarification but do not argue with the candidate.
- Avoid the danger of "side conversations" with one another.
- Be honest about the church.
- Know the duties, expectations, salary, and benefits of the position.
- Take notes.
- Treat all candidates fairly.
- Be clear about your time frame and your next steps.
- Never offer the position to a candidate during the interview.[13]

The manual of the Presbyterian Church (USA) *On Calling a Pastor* suggests the following interview questions:

- Tell us about your faith journey.
- What are the things you feel best about in your present ministry?
- What have been the challenges there?
- What makes you think you may be called to leave there now?
- What interests you about this position?

- What would you bring to our ministry?
- What are your greatest strengths in ministry? Your greatest weaknesses?
- One of our goals is to strengthen our _____ . How would you do that?
- Describe a typical week in your ministry.
- Share your perspectives on the Presbyterian Church (USA).
- One of the issues our session has debated in the past few years is _____ . Tell us how you might address that topic.
- If we selected you as our pastor, when could you start and what would be your start-up plan?
- How do you balance your personal/family life with your ministry?
- What will you need from the members of this church in order to be effective as our pastor?
- What are the financial concerns you have about possibly coming here?
- What questions or concerns do you have?[14]

Assign a committee member to give the candidate a tour of the church. Have him/her meet other members of the staff. Give a tour of the community to the candidate and any family members. Show them the retail section of the community as well as the residential sections. If the candidate has children, visit schools the children might attend.

Hearing Candidates Preach

The Search and Call Process in the United Church of Christ suggests that only candidates the search committee is seriously considering should be asked to preach in the church. In addition, the candidate should be asked to perform a task he/she would be performing on the job. If Sunday School teaching is a major duty, the candidate should teach a Sunday School class.[15]

One way to hear the candidate preach is to obtain the candidate's permission to visit the religious institution the candidate presently serves. There are other options. One is to arrange for the candidate to preach in a neutral pulpit in a different community. Another is to ask candidates to preach in your church on a day other than Sunday if they wish to preach in their own church on Sunday. Many candidates will need permission from the church that presently employs them to preach at your church on Sunday.

It is important for the congregation to have input. Congregants should be invited to hear all candidates preach. They should be given a biographic sketch of each candidate. Some churches schedule a session with the congregation to give the congregants an opportunity to ask questions of each candidate.

Inform the congregation in a letter, an e-mail or the church bulletin how congregants can provide comments to the search committee. For example, congregants might be given the e-mail address of the chair of the search committee with a due date for the receipt of comments.

Background Checks

Several faiths suggest that background checks be required for all candidates recommended for employment. This may include checks of employment, credit, criminal, and motor vehicle records. If the position will involve work with children, many states require specific background checks of individuals offered employment.

Selection of the Religious Leader

In some religions, the search committee makes its recommendations to the council, which in turn selects the candidate to be offered the position. The Conservative branch of the Jewish faith and many mosques follow this procedure. In the Baptist Church, the search committee recommends a candidate for pastor to the congregation. The prospective pastor is then invited to visit the church and preach to the congregation. The congregation votes on whether to offer the position to that candidate.[16]

One Unitarian Universalist church's by-laws provide that the ministerial candidate is hired upon approval by two-thirds of the voting members present at the Annual Meeting or a special congregational meeting held for the purpose of calling a minister. The quorum for such a meeting is 30 percent of the voting membership.[17]

Volunteer Religious Leader Is Selected

Many religions have volunteer religious leaders. The largest faith with volunteer religious leaders is the Church of Jesus Christ of Latter-Day Saints, or the Mormon Church.

Local congregations are called wards or branches. A stake is a group of local wards, similar to a diocese in a Catholic church. The spiritual leader of each ward is called the bishop, and the branch president for branches. As a member of the congregation who is volunteering in this position, he is unpaid and expected to earn his living outside the church. He does not require a degree in theology.

The Mormon Church has two priesthoods: the Aaronic Priesthood and the Melchizedek Priesthood. The Aaronic Priesthood is given to Mormon men aged 12 to 16 and to older men who are new converts. Bishops and stake presidents have the authority to confer the Melchizedek Priesthood by the laying of the hands. However, they can do this only with the common consent of the holders of the priesthood in the community. Once they have received the Melchizedek Priesthood, men are ordained to an office in the priesthood that carries specific responsibilities in the ward.[18]

Members of the Baha'i faith choose their volunteer leaders. A typical process in a community is to elect nine individuals to a Spiritual Assembly. These nine individuals carry out some of the responsibilities clergy play in other religions. They also assume the role an elected church council plays in other religions.[19]

In Wicca, there is no centralized organization. Some Wiccans join groups called covens; Wiccan traditions hold that the ideal number of members for a coven is 13. When being initiated into a coven, it is customary for an individual to study with the coven for a year and a day before dedicating himself/herself to the religion. Wiccans can be "promoted" into higher ranks such as head priestess or head priest, though some Wiccans work alone and are called solitary practitioners.[20]

Religions Without Religious Leaders

Some religions do not have a spiritual leader. For example, "unprogrammed worship" is the style of worship among the Religious Society of Friends, or Quakers. The Quaker faith relies heavily upon spiritual searching by individual members without the guidance of a pastor. Instead, meetings are held in silence until someone feels inspired to speak.

2

Supporting the Religious Leader

The duties of the minister are unique. There are some tasks only ministers can perform according to the laws and customs of their religious organizations. These duties should be noted in writing and understood by the minister, the council, and the congregation.

Yet, even though the minister has unique duties, it is important he/she has a supervisor, just as every employee of every organization should have a supervisor. Both the church and the minister can minimize conflicts if a single individual holds this supervisory position. In a church, it is appropriate for the minister's supervisor to be the council chair. In some congregations, another individual is designated as the minister's supervisor. All too often, no one supervises the minister; this leads to problems.

Executive Director or Church Administrator

Many large churches have an executive director or a church administrator. This is a professional with specific training and experience in managing a nonprofit organization. It is especially important to spell out the specific duties of the executive director and clearly differentiate them from the duties of the minister. Does the executive director report to the minister? Or does the minister report to the executive director? Who reports to the church council?

Of course, these two individuals must work closely together. It is important, however, to spell out individual responsibilities. Who hires and supervises the choir director or the principal of the school? Who hires the church secretary? Who supervises and gives assignments to the church secretary? To the building superintendent?

William G. Caldwell suggests the following job description for a pastor:

Principal Function: The pastor is responsible to the church to proclaim the gospel of Jesus Christ, to preach the biblical revelation, to engage in pastoral care ministries, to provide administrative leadership to all areas of church life, and to act as the chief administrator of the paid staff.

Responsibilities:

1. Plan and conduct the worship services; prepare and deliver sermons; lead in observance of ordinances.

2. Lead the church in an effective program of witnessing and in a caring ministry for persons in the church and community.

3. Visit members and prospects.

4. Conduct counseling sessions; perform wedding ceremonies; conduct funerals.

5. Lead the church in planning, organizing, directing, coordinating, and evaluating the total program of the church.

6. Work with deacons, church officers, and committees as they perform their assigned responsibilities.

7. Act as moderator of church business meetings (unless a lay person is elected as moderator).

8. Cooperate with denominational leaders in matters of mutual interest and concern; keep the church informed of denominational development; represent the church in civic matters.

9. Serve as chief administrator of the paid church staff; supervise the work of assigned paid staff workers.[1]

Meetings

It is important for churches to have regularly scheduled meetings. Here are some suggestions for possible meetings:

• The minister meets on a regular basis with the "senior staff." This would include the executive director, educational director, and music director. The council chair should attend this meeting, which is often held once a week.

- The minister and the executive director might meet once a month with the entire staff to review upcoming events.

- The council chair and the minister should meet on a regular basis to review the program schedule and discuss any problems they anticipate. In many churches, the council chair serves as the minister's supervisor. Their weekly meeting would include a review of the minister's schedule. Periodically, they would refer to the minister's job description to be sure it is current. They would set long-range plans for the minister's continuing education. They would discuss any problems the minister has in leading the congregation. The council chair and the minister would review the minister's latest task list to make certain it is still current. The task list should be as detailed as possible and should be updated regularly.

- In some churches, the system that works best is for the council chair to appoint a small "minister's liaison committee" to meet with the minister on a regular basis. The minister could then have confidential discussions with a small group of congregational leaders about issues that arise.

A critical part of any church is to have an excellent working relationship among the council, the minister, and the congregation. The council should not make any decision regarding the minister's duties without the council chair speaking with the minister first. The same courtesy should be extended by the minister. The minister should not make a decision affecting the church without discussing it with the council chair first.

Every effort should be made to discuss both present and potential conflicts. Some difficulties may be between the council and the minister; others may be between the congregation and the minister. In many situations, the minister and the council chair can minimize or diffuse conflicts by just discussing them.

One system for minimizing conflict is for every church to have two lists. One is a list that would include decisions the minister can make without council approval. A second list would include decisions the council can make without the minister's approval. When there is a possible conflict, these lists can be reviewed to indicate who has the final say on that particular issue.

It is important for as many aspects as possible of the minister's responsibilities and the council's responsibilities to be put in writing. This avoids numerous problems later on. Examples might include:

- If the minister lives in a home furnished by the congregation, what are the procedures for major and minor maintenance?

- When the minister leaves the congregation for any reason, how long does he/she have to vacate the home provided by the congregation?

- Does the minister get a sabbatical and, if so, for how long? Does the minister get paid during the sabbatical?

- When there is a life-cycle event such as a wedding or a funeral for a member of the congregation, does the minister charge the congregant for her/his services? If there is no charge but the congregant decides to send a check to the minister, is the minister permitted to use the funds as a personal contribution or should the contribution be used for church-related functions? Any charges for life-cycle events should be spelled out in writing.

Positive communications among the minister, the church council, and the congregation are essential if the church is to meet the needs of its members.

3

Evaluating the Religious Leader and Staff

The position of the minister is a critical one in any church. For many congregants, their relationship with the minister is an extremely important part of their lives. Each church needs to develop a system for a formal evaluation of the minister.

One excellent procedure is to establish a "minister liaison committee." This committee could consist of the council chair, the personnel committee chair, and one other parishioner. It should meet monthly with the minister. The meetings would be informal and would include discussions about how to help the church meet the needs of the parishioners. One important task of this committee would be to plan the minister's annual performance review. Because the minister is present when the procedures are developed, the possibility of miscommunication is lessened.

Quarterly Task List

One important part of the evaluation process is the development of a quarterly task list. Often, the minister develops the task list and reviews it with the personnel committee. A quarterly list might include:

- Attend regional ministers' conference and report recommendations to council at the March meeting.
- Review the Easter program with the choir director.
- Give book review of _____ on _____.
- Meet with the conversion class on _____.
- Lead adult education classes on _____.
- Review curriculum with educational director.

At the end of each quarter, the personnel committee meets with the minister. It reviews the objectives for the last quarter to see if they have been accomplished. It then discusses with the minister the objectives for the next quarter.

Ministry Review

An annual ministry review is important for every congregation. It gives the council an opportunity to list the minister's accomplishments and thank him/her for service to the congregation. All too often, a minister provides excellent service, but no written statement exists acknowledging this fact.

The ministry review process includes congregational input into the various ways the minister can serve the congregation. Members of the congregation may have specific suggestions for ways the minister can be of even greater assistance. Likewise, the minister can make recommendations to the council and the membership of steps that can be taken to improve the religious life of the congregation.

Here are the recommendations of the Presbyterian Church (USA):

> An important component of a healthy pastor-congregation relationship is the willingness to periodically assess the effectiveness of ministry with the recognition that ministry is a shared function of minister and members. Each year the pastor and the session need to evaluate how they have worked together to achieve their mutual goals for ministry during the preceding year. This facilitates a positive climate where the pastor and all church officers can make adjustments in allocating their energy and time as effectively as possible. Every three to five years, a session retreat or congregational mission study should be considered as a way to discern God's call to the congregation and the pastor for the next phase of their ministry together.[1]

Congregational Input

Each church should institute a formal system for congregants to have input into the evaluation of the minister. The church should have a system with which it feels comfortable. For example, the chair of the personnel committee would write to each congregant. The congregant should be informed that the minister receives a periodic evaluation and should be asked to help the personnel committee by taking the following survey:

Rate the minister's service to the congregation:

_____ Excellent _____ Good _____ Fair _____ Poor

Comments: _____

_____

Suggestions to improve the minister's service to the congregation:

_____

_____

Name (Optional) _____

Evaluation Period

The evaluation period should be determined on a case-by-case basis. A new minister should be evaluated after three months of service. Generally, a minister and all church employees should be evaluated each year. One exception is if major problems have been identified. Then, a shorter evaluation period—perhaps six months— should be set.

Evaluation Process

Before beginning the evaluation process, determine what would be most effective for your congregation. Review what has been done before. If the existing system has been effective, do not change it. It is often helpful to get advice from the judicatory serving your congregation. Sometimes, getting advice from other churches in your denomination may result in useful recommendations as well. The Presbyterian format is a good one to follow:

> An annual performance review of the pastor's service in the light of the ministry goals of the congregation should be conducted by the Personnel Committee of the Session. This is an opportunity for the pastor to get significant constructive feedback about his or her practice of ministry, to discuss weaknesses or new competencies needed, and to develop a plan for the minister's continuing education for the coming year that will address those issues. Ministry and performance reviews should take place before the compensation

review or the unique purpose of each is lost. Too often money becomes the focus or the weapon and other issues are not dealt with constructively.[2]

The evaluation of the minister should be conducted by the church's personnel committee. This committee should be composed of individuals who have the respect of the entire congregation. The council chair should be invited to participate.

The evaluation has six parts:

1. Review of job description. When the minister is hired, he/she is given a job description. At each evaluation, the job description is reviewed to make certain it is still current. New tasks should be added; tasks no longer being performed should be deleted.

2. Review of current year's task list. At the beginning of each year, the minister and the personnel committee agree on a list of objectives for the year. The list should be as specific as possible and should include deadlines for the accomplishment of each task. As the year progresses, the task list is revised as needed. At each evaluation session, the minister and the personnel committee should review the task list approved at the last meeting. For example, if the evaluation is an annual one, the task list the minister and the personnel committee agreed to a year before should be reviewed. Were all the tasks accomplished satisfactorily? If not, why not?

3. Review of quarterly task lists. Many councils and ministers find the development of quarterly task lists to be an effective tool. The notes from previous sessions with the minister to discuss previous quarterly task lists would be reviewed.

4. Review of comments by congregants. The comments received by the members of the congregation should be reviewed. If there are many, they can be summarized; if there are few, they can be discussed individually. Make certain to keep the recommendations confidential.

5. Review of comments by the minister liaison committee. This group will have met with the minister once a

month and should be able to have important input into the evaluation process.

6. Preparation of new task list. The minister and personnel committee then agree on a task list for the next year.

Once the meeting is over, the personnel committee gives the minister a written report. It thanks him/her for service to the congregation and is as specific as possible about positive achievements during the previous evaluation period. If there are any areas to be improved, they are outlined in as specific terms as possible. Deadlines for improvement should be stated. The task list for the next evaluation period should be attached.

Jill M. Hudson, in her book *When Better Isn't Enough: Evaluation Tools for the 21st Century Church,* recommends 12 characteristics of an effective 21st-century pastor:

1. The ability to maintain personal, professional, and spiritual balance.
2. The ability to guide a transformational faith experience.
3. The ability to motivate and develop a congregation to be a "mission outpost."
4. The ability to develop and communicate a vision.
5. The ability to interpret and lead change.
6. The ability to promote and lead spiritual formation for church members.
7. The ability to provide leadership for high-quality, relevant worship experiences.
8. The ability to identify, develop, and support lay leaders.
9. The ability to build, inspire, and lead a staff/volunteer team.
10. The ability to manage conflict.
11. The ability to navigate successfully the world of technology.
12. The ability and desire to be a lifelong learner.

Hudson's book walks the personnel committee through a process for evaluating the minister in these 12 areas.[3]

All books and articles on evaluating the minister suggest this should be a positive process for the minister, the personnel committee, and the congregation. Indeed, David R. Pollock, in his book *Business Management in the Local Church* states "a pastor should welcome an opportunity to be evaluated."[4]

Pollock's reasoning is compelling:

Here is an opening to invite church leaders into the world of ministry. He could share with them the long hours spent in sermon preparation, hospital visitation, counseling, administrative details, and late-night phone calls. And don't forget those emotional burdens. Officiating at the funeral of a child, counseling a distraught wife, trying to save a failing marriage, always having to be the cheerleader, the pressure to preach inspiring messages, and making those heartfelt appeals to meet the budget. This is a chance to show your leaders that shepherding is more than preaching a Sunday message. It's a golden opportunity to ask them to pray with you and for you.[5]

The evaluation process for other paid staff members—religious school principal, teachers, choir leader—is conducted by these individuals' supervisors. The process is similar to the minister's evaluation in that it begins with a review of that staff member's job description and an update, if necessary. The task list for the evaluation period is then reviewed to see if the tasks were all conducted satisfactorily. The supervisor and the staff member then agree on the task list for the next evaluation period. As with the minister, each staff member receives a written evaluation report. It thanks him/her for service during the evaluation period. If there are any areas to be improved, they are outlined in as specific terms as possible. If possible, deadlines for improvement are stated. The task list for the next evaluation period is attached.

For both the minister and the other church employees, the evaluation process should be a positive experience. Every evaluation meeting should begin with praising and thanking the individual for service to the congregation. In many cases, the employee outlines specific areas in which change is needed, so even this part of the evaluation process is constructive. Remember at all times the purpose of the evaluation process is to improve the church. How can each employee contribute to that process?

An excellent summary of the entire evaluation process is provided by George H. Hunter in *Leading and Managing a Growing Church*:

> There are several well-known "secrets" for effective performance appraisals: (A) Give your people frequent, informal feedback upon performance—so that there will be no new agendas or "surprises" in the more formal performance appraisal, but only a more structured conversation of matters already discussed informally. (B) Base the conversation upon performance in relation to the mutually agreed upon standards, outcomes, and indicators. (C) Use both the frequent informal conversations and the less frequent formal performance appraisals as opportunities to positively reinforce what the person is doing effectively. Where constructive critique is needed, do not focus upon or attack the person, but upon specific behaviors and their counterproductive effects upon the manager and/or the organization. (D) Lawrence Appley reminds us that "the main purpose of an appraisal of an individual should be to discover what can be done...to help him develop his greatest potential." So, effective leaders do not use the performance appraisal primarily to dwell upon past performance, and especially past failures, but to learn from the past experience while focusing primarily upon the future and what the person will do to achieve objectives. (E) If termination, or placement in some other role, is very clearly warranted, a quick thorough incision is more humane and effective than cutting away inch by inch over time. Effective leaders do not try to make a subordinate's life miserable, hoping they will resign. They explain the reasons for the decision, they suggest the kind of job the person could do more effectively, they offer to facilitate the person's placement into a role that better fits his or her aptitude, and they give the person the opportunity to resign.[6]

Remember that the evaluation process should be a positive process rather than a punitive one. It should be used as an opportunity to praise employees for positive work and to focus constructively on areas that could be improved.

4

Firing the Religious Leader

Divorcing a spouse is a traumatic event. No matter how much you try to reduce the trauma, it still exists. Similarly, every congregation that fires its religious leader experiences a great deal of pain in the process. The best a church can do is to try to minimize the difficulties.

Begin by patiently taking every step you can to improve the minister's performance, rather than resorting to firing the minister. See Chapter 3 for ways to do this. When all else fails and the congregation decides to terminate the minister's services, several steps can be taken to reduce the trauma.

In many faiths, it is the responsibility of the council to both hire and fire the minister. It is important to include in the by-laws specific procedures to be followed for ending the minister's service to the congregation. For example, what input does the congregation have in the decision? What notice must the church give the minister before the termination? If the minister has a contract to serve the congregation for a period of years, it may be appropriate to take a confidential survey of congregants as to whether the contract terms should be extended.

Make certain to review the roles of the regional judicatory and denominational national office before taking action to fire a minister. These offices can often provide excellent advice. It is important to obtain the support of these bodies before the separation occurs.

Consult with an attorney who specializes in personnel matters and advises about following the law and minimizing hard feelings and controversy. The attorney will review the original agreement to hire the minister as well as the church's personnel policies.

The attorney will also advise about laws regarding giving notice and hearings, and inform council members of the rules regarding confidentiality. What information regarding termination of a minister may be shared with the congregation? How do the council and the congregation deal with the problems that arise when the minister does not tell the truth about the reasons for the termination? When should possible criminal behavior be reported to law enforcement authorities? How should council members reply when asked by possible new employers for information about the minister's performance? How should the council chair reply when contacted by a newspaper reporter asking questions about the minister's termination?

One recommendation is not to use the word *fire*. If the minister has a contract with the congregation that will not be renewed, just inform the congregation that the contract will not be renewed. If the council definitely votes to terminate the minister's services, it is courteous to give the minister an opportunity to resign rather than being fired. If the minister does resign, it is important not to reveal that the minister was asked to resign. The specific reasons for the firing must remain confidential. Council members must pledge not to share information about the action with anyone. The notice about the council action should be given to the minister by the council chair or the chair of the personnel committee in person. It should then be followed up by a written notice to the minister. Try to make this difficult task as sensitive as possible.

In some religious faiths, the congregation may vote to "discharge" the minister. Here are provisions from the by-laws of a Unitarian Universalist Church:

The Minister will be discharged if:

1. At a properly called congregational meeting, a majority of qualified members vote to discharge. For the purpose of this section, a quorum exists if 50 percent of the qualified membership is present.

2. If a quorum is not achieved, the Minister can elect to waive the quorum requirement and proceed to a binding vote, following opportunity for discussion.

3. Should the Minister decide not to waive the quorum requirement, then the members present will be allowed to discuss the motion to discharge the Minister. At the end of the meeting, their votes shall be recorded on individual ballots and given to the Clerk, who shall hold them in strict confidence. As soon as possible, the Clerk will mail ballots to the remaining members, who will be afforded two weeks from the date of mailing to return their votes to the Clerk.

4. The outcome of the voting will be announced in church on the Sunday immediately following the due date for votes. The Clerk shall not reveal the result of any vote or provide any vote tallies until the final result is announced in church. The result will be binding.[1]

The Baptist faith document states that "A pastor serves in the church as long as both pastor and congregation agree the relationship should continue."[2]

In many situations, the judicatory may have rule regarding termination of a religious leader. For example, the United Synagogue of Conservative Judaism publishes "The USCJ Guide to Contractual Relations." The Guide begins by stating in bold print that the Guide is not legally binding on any congregation and the specific agreement between the congregation and the clergy and professional staff applies.[3] Later in the document, the Guide states that "It is strongly recommended" that if a rabbi's services are terminated by the congregation, even it is simply the end of a contractual term and the congregation chooses not to renew, the Rabbi be given severance pay according to a specific plan.[4] However, what congregations find is, despite the "voluntary" language of the "Guide," these rules and others in the document are often mandatory. In this branch of Judaism, congregations can interview only rabbis sent to them by the judicatory.

A number of additional steps should be taken to reduce the pain of any separation:

- The council chair should send a letter to each congregant giving the necessary information in as sensitive a manner as possible. Begin by thanking the minister for service to the congregation. Then simply state the fact that the minister has submitted his/her resignation or that the council has decided not to renew the minister's contract with the congregation. That is all that is needed. No more specific information should be given to the congregation, either in writing or otherwise.

- Give the minister a termination notice long before his or her salary will stop. Because it will take the minister some time to find a new position and for the congregation to hire a new minister, a long notice will benefit both parties.

- Give the minister a generous severance package. You want to minimize the minister's financial pain. It is common in some religions to give the minister two weeks' severance pay if he/she has served less than two years and one week's pay for every year of service if he/she has served more than two years. Remember that ministers are not covered under governmental unemployment compensation programs, so be generous.

- Give the minister enough lead time to apply for other positions.

- Inform the minister that the council will keep the specific reasons for the firing confidential and you expect that he/she will extend the same courtesy to the congregation.

- Be very sensitive in thanking the minister for service to the congregation.

- Certainly a special prayer at a service wishing the minister well in his/her future position would be in order.

William G. Caldwell provides specific "termination procedures":

1. Voluntary Termination

    a. Two (2) weeks written notification must be given prior to the effective date of resignation. Failure to make proper notification could result in the loss of any accumulated benefits.

    b. In the case of called staff, the resignation must be announced at a church meeting.

2. Involuntary Termination

    a. Any church employee may be terminated involuntarily for unsatisfactory performance, failure to support church programs, failure to adhere to established personnel procedures or behavior unbecoming a Christian (as determined by vote of the church).

    b. Support staff may be terminated by his/her supervisor with the approval of the Personnel Committee.

    c. Called staff members may be terminated by the church. Such action may be initiated by the pastor and the Personnel Committee.

    d. Called staff terminated involuntarily may be given up to three (3) months severance pay and benefits as determined by the personnel committee.[5]

Carefully think through how to be sensitive during the termination process, for the sake of both the minister and the congregation. It is important to have a discussion with the minister about ways to make the parting as painless as possible for both sides.

The Council

Policy for religious organizations is usually set by a board of volunteers, the same as with boards of other nonprofit organizations. Councils of churches differ widely. It is important for parishioners to learn how the particular council of their church operates.

Name and Duties

Groups can be called councils, boards, boards of trustees, advisory boards, sessions, and numerous other names.

Be certain to learn the exact responsibilities of the council of your church, synagogue, mosque, or temple. In some churches, the duties are set by the judiciary, such as the synod or presbytery. In others, the church membership sets the duties. Many councils are "governing boards." They are the body legally responsible for running the church. Usually, two major responsibilities of governing boards are hiring staff and setting the budget.

Contact the regional judiciary and your denomination's national office regarding congregational constitutions and by-laws. Some religious traditions have models of these official documents in which certain parts are mandatory and other aspects are optional.

An often-controversial section is called the Reversionary Provision, which states who gets church property in the event of a conflict or dissolution of the congregation.

Some churches have "advisory boards," which are responsible for advising the minister on operating the church. Each parish in a Catholic Church establishes a Pastoral Council. The pastor heads the Council, and the purpose of the Council is to advise the pastor.[1]

One church lists the duties of the council as follows:

- Help the church understand its mission and define its priorities.
- Coordinate studies of church and community needs.
- Recommend to the church coordinated plans for evangelism, missions, Christian development, worship, stewardship, and ministry.
- Coordinate the church's schedule of activities, special events, and use of facilities.
- Evaluate progress and the priority use of church resources. In most churches, this group would be chaired by the pastor and would include:
  - Church staff members.
  - Leaders of all church programs and ministry organizations.
  - Leader of the deacons (or church board).
  - Chairpersons of key committees (those closely related to the work of church programs and ministries, such as missions, stewardship, and nominating committees).[2]

Selecting Members

In many churches with councils, the council is responsible for selecting its own members. In other churches, the full congregation selects the council members.

The usual method for finding council members is not the most effective way to find excellent members. Under the system commonly used, a nominating committee is established. It meets once a year to recommend council members. The discussion is "Whom do you know?" Once some names are recommended, often the chair calls these individuals and says, "This is Bill. I chair the church nominating committee and your name was recommended to serve on the council. Please agree to serve. You will receive a notice of our next meeting."

A more effective method of recruiting excellent council members is the establishment of a council development committee, a standing committee of the church that meets several times during the year. Find a chair who has the respect of all segments of church membership. Ideally that individual would be someone who knows most of the members of the congregation and what they could contribute to the council. In many organizations, either by tradition or as a by-law provision, the immediate past chair of the council serves as the chair of the council development committee.

Recommending Members and Officers

One major responsibility of this committee is to recommend council members and officers. The council development committee should meet several months in advance of the meeting at which the recommended slate would be presented. The committee should review the present council members to see whether they have met their responsibilities as council members:

- What is their attendance record at council meetings?
- Did they make an appropriate financial commitment to the church?
- Were they regular attendees at church services?
- Did they chair a committee, sit on a committee, and fulfill other requirements of council membership?
- Did they make constructive recommendations at council meetings?

Council members who fulfilled their duties should be asked if they would be willing to serve another term. If they have not been excellent, do not nominate them for another term. (Make certain, however, to thank all council members for their service.)

The council development committee should attempt to nominate individuals to help ensure a diverse mix of church members on the council:

- Age.
- Young singles.
- Young parents.
- Empty nesters.
- Income ranges.
- Long-term church members.
- New church members.
- Ethnic backgrounds.

Lists of Potential Council Members

Begin an open process of asking for potential council members:

- Put a notice in the church bulletin asking individuals who are interested in serving on the council to contact the chair of the council development committee.
- Ask the chairs of other committees to recommend active members of their committees.
- Ask the minister for names of possible council members.
- Ask existing council members for names of possible council members.
- Consider all the church's office and program volunteers.

Once a potential council member is identified, that individual should be interviewed in person by a member of the council development committee. The potential council member is given a list of duties that would include:

- Attendance at the council orientation program.
- Attendance at all council meetings.
- Regular attendance at church services.
- Active participation on at least one church standing committee.
- A financial contribution to the church.
- Attendance at all church major special events.

Potential council members who do not agree to perform these duties should not be asked to join the council.

Orientation

It is essential to have an orientation session for all new council members before they attend their first council meeting. Well before the orientation, each new member should be given a packet. The packet would include:

- By-laws.
- Minutes of last several council meetings.
- Most recent audit.

- List of all committees (chair, duties, minutes).
- Job descriptions of major staff members.
- Names and positions of all major staff members.
- Names, addresses, phone numbers, and e-mail addresses of all current council members.
- Existing policies, such as personnel and fiscal policies.
- Church brochure.
- History of the church and the denomination.
- Statement of church beliefs.

The orientation session should be led by the council chair. The agenda could be as follows:

- Prayer led by the minister.
- Introduction of staff members.
- Introduction of council members.
- Introduction of new council members.
- Review of the packet.
- Responsibilities of council members.
- Council meeting procedures.
- Closing benediction by the minister.

Planning for Council Meetings

Planning for council meetings should begin several weeks before each meeting. The council chair, minister, and executive director should meet in person to develop the agenda for the meeting. By this time, all committee reports and the minutes of the last council meeting should have been submitted.

The minutes of the last meeting should be reviewed to see which issues should be included on the agenda. The council packet should be e-mailed or sent by U.S. mail to all council members at least a week before the meeting. The packet should contain the following items:

- Tentative agenda.
- Minutes of last council meeting.
- Treasurer's report.
- Committee reports.

- Council chair's report.
- Minister's report.

If council members have any additional items for the agenda, they should notify the chair by e-mail at least two days before the council meeting. Council members should be informed that if they are not attending the meeting, they must notify the council chair by e-mail or telephone.

The Council Meeting

Council meetings should begin on time. There is no better way to encourage members to be on time than to start the meetings on time. The meeting should begin with the distribution of the agenda. An order of business might include the following:

- Prayer.
- Religious teaching.
- Request for additional agenda items.
- Minutes of last meeting.
- Treasurer's report.
- Committee reports. If there are any motions to be made, they should be in written form at the end of the committee report.
- Chair's report. This would cover items brought to the attention of the chair at the beginning of the meeting. There should be no additional items of new business raised at the meeting.
- Executive director's report.
- Minister's report.
- Old business (items specifically held over from previous meetings).
- Good and welfare.
- Opportunity for announcements, general suggestions, input from non-council members.
- Adjournment.
- Refreshments.

The council serves the congregation, so a number of steps should be taken to emphasize this point:

- A list of the dates and times of all council meetings should be included in the church bulletin.
- All council meetings should be open to all congregation members.
- Congregants who wish to address the council should ask the council chair for permission.
- Periodically, in the church bulletin or in a separate mailing, the council chair should inform the congregation of decisions that were made at each council meeting.
- Minutes of all council meetings may be reviewed by any congregational member.
- Individuals who would like to serve on the council should make their request known to the chair of the council development committee.

Meeting Rules and Procedures

It is recommended that a church council should use the "strong chair" method of governance. When an item is raised at a council meeting, the chair decides how it should be handled.

The chair has numerous options:

- If an item can be disposed of quickly, the chair may bring it up immediately.
- The chair may refer the issue to the appropriate committee and ask the chair of that committee to bring a recommendation to the next council meeting.
- The chair may create an ad hoc committee to review the issue and bring a recommendation to the next council meeting.
- If the item has a religious component, the chair may ask the minister to review it.
- The chair may postpone the issue in order to obtain information about how other churches handle it.

If a controversial issue is coming up, the chair states the recommendation of the committee or staff member who has reviewed it. The standard procedure is to begin with a motion, which is seconded. The chair may then set rules for the discussion. For example, the chair may decide that two individuals may speak for the motion and two against and may set time limits on the discussion

The aim of any discussion at a church council is to achieve consensus. The chair will offer a compromise if one is possible. If additional study is needed, the chair will postpone the item until the next meeting. Every effort should be taken not to have a close vote on any issue. One technique the chair can use is to take a "straw" or unofficial vote to see what the preliminary views of the council members are. If the council is unanimous on an issue, there is no reason for further discussion.

Most authors are quick to recommend church councils avoid using Robert's Rules of Order. Dan Hotchkiss, in *Governance and Ministry,* points out that Henry Martyn Robert wrote his rules in 1876 after trying unsuccessfully to chair an unruly meeting of his church. However, Hotchkiss argues, "his rules fall short of modern boards' requirements."[3]

Shawchuck and Hueser, in their book *Managing the Congregation,* were even more emphatic: "Perhaps the most damaging invention ever made to squelch creative group discernment is Robert's Rules of Order—and the vote."[4]

Robert's Rules are complex and are useful in halls such as Congress where contentiousness is the rule and the majority decides. Churches, however, should follow the "consensus model" of governing. The chair leads a discussion on a topic. If there is not a unanimous or near-unanimous agreement on a topic, no action should be taken.

The council should adopt its own rules of order and follow them. I recommended the following rules of order for an organization I chaired:

SAND'S RULES OF ORDER

A. No document longer than one page gets handed out at a meeting. Documents longer than a page are mailed or e-mailed to each member prior to the meeting.

B. Nothing gets read aloud at a board meeting. All items are duplicated and distributed to the board members.

C. If a committee has met, its report is in writing and is distributed to the board members before the meeting.

D. Reports of the executive director, other staff, and consultants are in writing, and are distributed in advance of the meeting.

E. No important item gets discussed at a board meeting without someone having thought about it before. Some items might have been reviewed by a committee before being discussed at a board meeting. Other items might have been carefully reviewed by the board chair or the executive director. If a board member raises an item at a meeting that has not been reviewed prior to the discussion, the board chair refers that matter to the appropriate committee or individual.

F. As items are raised at the board meeting, the chair states if the item requires the setting of board policy. If policy-making, a board member is asked to make a motion before a discussion is held. If the matter requires implementation only, no motion is made. Once the discussion has ended, the issue is referred to the executive director for appropriate staff action.

G. As procedural items are raised at a board meeting, the board chair decides what steps should be followed. The chair might refer an item to a committee, for example, or set a time limit for debate of a particular item. The only time a vote is taken on a procedural item is if a board member requests such a vote.

H. Rules of order are used to help, not to disrupt. The board chair tries to avoid the use of rules to complicate rather than simplify the board decision-making process.

I. All votes are by a simultaneous show of hands. When the board chair requests a vote on a motion, the request is for all in favor to raise their hand and then for all opposed to raise their hand. The secretary can then record the votes.

J. When there is unanimous consent to a board action, no separate vote is taken. The board chair will state: "Do I hear any objection to the motion? If not, the secretary will note unanimous approval."[5]

Hotchkiss recommends one other important technique to shorten meetings significantly. This "consent agenda" technique was instituted long after Robert wrote his rules. When the board chair and the executive director or minister get together to plan the agenda, they divide the items into those that are likely to generate discussion and those that are very unlikely to generate discussion. All the latter items are listed under the "consent agenda."

Hotchkiss gives examples including approval of the minutes, signing a contract for a project the board has already approved, shifting money from one budget to another, empowering the treasurer to open a new bank account, adjusting deductibles on an insurance policy, and updating personnel policies to conform to new laws.[6] Only one vote is taken on all of the items on the consent agenda.

Council Meeting Attendance

It is especially important to have full attendance at council meetings. Because many topics are discussed at several consecutive meetings, attending all meetings is necessary.

Inform prospective council members that attendance at meetings is mandatory. If they indicate they cannot promise monthly attendance, do not put them on the council. Also, tell them that if they find their situation changes and they cannot continue to attend all meetings, they should resign from the council.

If council members must miss a particular meeting, ask them to send an e-mail ahead of time to the council chair. That way, the chair can ask individuals who will not be attending their views about particular issues that might arise. The chair also will know for sure how many packets to prepare. Council members who miss any meetings without informing the council chair of their non-attendance should be sent a note under the signature of the council chair reminding them of the attendance rule.

If a council member misses a second consecutive meeting without an excuse, the member should receive a phone call from either the council chair or the chair of the council development committee. The member should be reminded of the by-law provision that council members who miss three consecutive meetings automatically forfeit their council seats. Council members who miss three consecutive meetings without an excuse automatically should receive a note signed by the council secretary informing them they are no longer on the council.

Dealing With Conflict

As Larry Osborne asks in *Sticky Teams*, "What is it about board meetings that brings out the worst in us?"[7] Osborne's "Five Major Roadblocks to Unity" provide a good place to start:

- Meeting in the wrong place.
- Ignoring relationships.
- Not meeting often enough.
- Constant turnover.
- Too many members.[8]

Osborne offers a possible way to begin to solve the problem. Hold one meeting specifically and exclusively to discuss church governance. Invite the council members, the minister, and some non-council congregants to a meeting whose topics are "improving church unity." No business is allowed. Invite an individual who is skilled in solving conflict problems to lead the meeting.

Identify the problems in your church (which may be different than the ones Osborne lists). Ask the minister for guidance on how conflicts were resolved in that religion's scriptures or traditions. Discuss specific ways of lessening conflict.

Dealing With Difficult Council Members

Dealing with difficult council members may be especially hard in a religious setting. One of the principles of religious groups is kindness to others. Trying to be kind to a fellow board member who is disruptive or unpleasant is not easy to do.

Generally, embarrassing individuals by criticizing their behavior at a public meeting is not appropriate. However, there are certain behaviors such as profanity and name-calling that should be stopped immediately. Sometimes, inappropriate behavior can be stopped by an excellent council chair in ways that will not embarrass the offending member. These may include:

- Putting a time limit on all comments and enforcing it.
- Asking individuals to speak only about the motion on the floor.

- Insisting that members address the chair and not each other.

- Having a statement in the by-laws that certain types of speech are not permitted, such as profanity.

If a council member continues to act inappropriately, document exactly what the inappropriate behavior was. The council chair should speak to the individual privately.

The chair should state what the behavior was, rather than characterizing it as inappropriate or unacceptable. The chair in as kind a voice as possible should tell the individual how to handle a similar situation the next time it comes up at a meeting.

Dealing With a Difficult Council Chair

In a church setting, it is especially hard to deal with a difficult council chair. Because an ineffective council chair makes it difficult for other council members to act effectively, however, action must be taken. It is important not to embarrass the council chair in public. Try to avoid this at all costs.

Check the by-laws to see when the term of the council chair ends. If the term ends relatively soon, when the chair of the council development committee asks for officer recommendations, send a confidential note suggesting that the present chair not be re-nominated. If the chair has several months left to serve, other measures must be taken. How can the chair's performance be improved without embarrassing either the chair or the church? Often, a meeting of the officers or the executive committee is a good place to have a discussion of the chair's performance. First, have one of the officers carefully document the problem and suggest a possible solution. For example, if the chair does not have effective skills to lead the council meeting, one of the council members with the necessary experience or an outside consultant can work privately with the chair to improve his/her skills.

If the chair uses inappropriate speech, give the chair examples of this speech and recommendations for appropriate words to use instead. In extreme situations, such as when the chair's behavior is so inappropriate that there is a real danger that board members will stop attending board meetings, the officers or the executive committee should ask for the chair's resignation.

Roles of Council Members and Staff

One common problem with a church council is confusion with regard to council and staff roles. In a traditional nonprofit agency, the board sets policy for the organization and the staff carries it out. Many church council members serve on the boards of nonprofits in the community. They are comfortable with coming to a monthly meeting and setting policy.

However, even in large churches, council members perform staff roles—the "doing"—in addition to traditional board roles—setting policy. Council members are called on to perform many responsibilities including selling tickets, cooking food, and writing press releases. These are staff functions, and so the confusion begins. Does the church executive director as a staff member give instructions to a council member who has volunteered to help in the church office, or docs the council member give instructions to the executive director or church secretary?

Other complications arise in church governance. Who supervises the minister? Are there some decisions the minister can make about church policy without council approval? Who supervises the executive director? Does the minister? The council?

Larry Osborne argues that "One of the best ways to cut off disharmony and dysfunction at the pass is to clarify board roles and staff roles before someone joins the team...."[9] He states, "A ministry can't remain healthy and vibrant when behind-the-scenes turf battles, budget wars, and volunteer raids are taking place. Fiefdoms and silos might make for strong programming, but the price is a sick church."[10]

Numerous problems are created when it is not decided and stated in writing ahead of time who can make which decisions. For example, what if the council wants to change the time of services (or the content or the length) and the minister says no? Who wins?

Also, there are no right or wrong answers. Two churches will come up with two different solutions, and neither is correct or incorrect. Churches with many staff members will come up with different models than those with a few staff members. Other factors that may influence a decision could include the number of parishioners and the traditions in that church.

One model is outlined in the *Book of Order of the Presbyterian Church (USA)*. It outlines the responsibilities of the minister and those of the council (session):

The minister as pastor has certain responsibilities which are not subject to the authority of the session. In a particular service of worship the pastor is responsible for:

1. The selection of Scripture lessons to be read.

2. The presentation and preaching of the sermon or exposition of the Word.

3. The prayers offered on behalf of the people and those prepared for the use of the people in worship.

4. The music to be sung.

5. The use of drama, dance, and other art forms.[11]

The book also states:

The session has authority:

*   To oversee and approve all public worship in the life of the particular church with the exception of those responsibilities delegated to the pastor alone.

*   To determine occasions, days, times, and places for worship.[12]

Don Hotchkiss recommends a workable solution to the problem of council members playing both board and staff roles. He calls this the "hat" solution. "Each hat represents a different kind of activity: a board member has a board hat, but if he is a tenor in the choir, he takes his board hat off and wears his choir hat to rehearsals." So here, the choir director gives instructions to the council member who sings in the choir.[13]

Larry Osborne offers another management tool that can be used specifically by church councils. He suggests that in addition to the monthly council meeting, the council should have a second meeting with only three purposes:

*   Team building.
*   Training.
*   Prayer.[14]

No votes. No business decisions. No minutes. He calls it a "Shepherds' Meeting," but obviously the name can be changed to fit the religious tradition of a particular church.

I would like to add a fourth item to the agenda of the Shepherds' Meeting. Discussions could be held at this meeting in an unhurried manner about the role of the church. In a jam-packed monthly business meeting, there never is adequate time to discuss very important issues. The topic for a church Shepherds' Meeting might be "What did Jesus tell us about helping the poor?" A synagogue discussion might be "How should we relate to intermarried children or friends in the community?" A mosque discussion might be "How do we correct the misinformation about Muslims in the general community?"

Open Council Meetings

All council meetings should be open to members of the congregation. Some congregations provide a period before the official meeting is called to order for general members to make short statements to the council. Others do not let non-council members speak unless they have submitted a written request to the council chair. One common practice of councils is to call an executive session for personnel and legal matters. Only council members as well as selected staff members invited by the council can attend these sessions.

Lessening Conflict

One important topic for consideration is how to avoid, or at least lessen, council conflict. "Baptist Congregation Church Governance: A Challenge" states, "The majority of major church conflicts arise over the issue of leadership, and many of these erupt when a pastor tries to control. Often these conflicts result in the dismissal of the pastor. Church splits also occur over this issue."[15] On the other hand, the document also states that the minister may not be the source of the discord, or even the deacons or elders claiming authority, but a few members of the church who wish to gain power. As the document states, "Whenever a few persons gain control, congregational governance flounders."[16] The Baptist document also points to apathy and indifference as causes of board problems. Every Baptist should play a part in improving church governance, it argues.

A comprehensive article on dealing with difficult people by Robert D. Dale not only gives practical advice but also divides difficult congregants into six categories:

A general strategy for coping effectively with difficult persons must be broad-based and constructive. Consider these actions:

- Pinpoint the problem. What exactly is the issue that's calling out the controller(s) and creating the tension in the congregation?
- Rate the relationship. How strong are the ties between the controller(s) and the leaders of the congregation?
- Count the cost of negative behavior within the congregation. Can the controlling actions be ignored, or must they be confronted?
- Search for a solution. What options are available for dealing with controlling behaviors?
- Covenant for continuity. Can an agreement be reached that will allow the congregation to advance toward its ultimate mission?

Each of the difficult persons mentioned displays controlling actions differently. *Hostiles*, for example, control their groups by daring to "be bad" in an institution that has a "nice" self-image. Their belligerence and demanding confrontiveness set the emotional tone for relating. If we avoid conflict or naively assume that hostiles will eventually ease the tension, we give the hostiles an important measure of control.

Cliques control a congregation's atmosphere for good or ill. Negatively, cliques gather for protection, revenge, or warfare. Positively, cliques lend status or share information with their members.

Crazy makers control communication processes by changing the subject, overloading the conversation with multiple issues, and contradicting. When we try to communicate with crazy makers, we are thrown off balance and feel "crazy." Crazy makers cause us to feel uncertain; therefore, they maintain leverage over us.

Apathetics exercise control in two passive modes. They withhold energy from the congregation's goals. They divide a congregation's focus between internal ministry to the apathetics themselves and outreach to others.

Lonelies control the attempts of others to build relationships by seeming to invite friendship and then holding others at arm's length. Additionally, they control many well-meaning helpers who develop a guilty conscience when their relationship-building efforts don't work.

Traditionalists worship the past so much they try to control a congregation's future. They seek to preserve by resisting all but emergency changes.[17]

General Suggestions for Improving Church Councils

An article that gives excellent suggestions for membership on a church council is "Welcome to The Board: A Practical How To Guide for Church Board Members" by R.W.P. Patterson.[18]

I agree with some of Mr. Patterson's recommendations:

- There are numerous board models. "A good rule is *to use the simplest organization structure* that works best for your church."[19]
- Churches may consider the "loose consensus" model for decision-making rather than voting.
- The most important requirements for any board member are a strong commitment to the mission and vision of the church and a desire to support the minister.

However, I disagree with Patterson on the following points:

- Patterson states that six to eight board members is a good number of council members to get an open discussion and a good representation of the church body. My experience is that most churches need many more than eight council members so that different ages, ethnic groups, incomes, and other diversities can be represented.
- Although the minister is the equivalent of the chief executive officer, I disagree that "the pastor is responsible

for everything that happens or fails to happen in the church."[20] The governing board of the church is responsible. The minister should report to the council and not the other way around.

- Patterson states that the minister sets goals and direction for the church. I submit that the minister should recommend goals and direction for the church and the church board should review, discuss, and implement them.

What is critically important is for the council itself to discuss any disagreements in a courteous and respectful way. In many situations, the council can turn to the holy books of that faith to gain insights on how to avoid dissention and discord. Following the teachings of your faith sets an excellent model for your church and its members.

6

Meaningful By-Laws

All too often, no one looks at the congregation's by-laws until there is a problem or even a crisis. Many times, a church does not even follow its own by-laws. Or worse yet, no one remembers where the by-laws even are. The council chair should bring the by-laws to every council meeting. They should be referred to frequently as issues arise. Creating and following meaningful by-laws creates a structure that effectively serves your organization.

General Provisions

A by-laws committee should be created and should meet at least once a year to review the by-laws. The committee should submit its recommendations in writing to the church council. The members of the congregation should be asked if they would like to suggest any changes to the by-laws. A process for making changes to the by-laws should be created.

Church Membership

The by-laws should state clearly who is eligible to be a member of the congregation. What are the criteria for membership? Does the council decide who is a member or does the congregation? What is the role of the minister in deciding who is a member?

Is membership by individual or by family? What if a wife is an adherent of the religion of the church but the husband is not? Can both be members? What about the children? Does it matter if the children are being brought up in the mother's faith or the father's? What are the rights of membership? Who can vote at congregational meetings? Who is eligible for attendance in Sunday School or in the congregational youth groups? These policies should be stated clearly in the by-laws.

Hiring the Religious Leader

Procedures for hiring the religious leader should be spelled out in the by-laws. See Chapter 1 for a description of numerous options.

Hiring an Executive Director

Many large churches have an executive director or church administrator. This individual serves as the professional manager for the church. Procedures for hiring the executive director should be outlined in the by-laws.

It is important that the executive director has a detailed job description, which is approved by the council. Make certain to state in writing which responsibilities are those of the executive director and which are those of the religious leader. Many churches have conflicts between the executive director and the minister as to who is responsible for what. You do not want your church to have these problems.

Hiring Other Staff Members

It is a good idea for all job descriptions to be approved by the council. This might include job descriptions of the educational director, secretary, bookkeeper, teachers, and music director. Spell out in the by-laws whether these individuals are to be hired by the council, the executive director, or the minister. State who is supervisor for each position.

Council Size

There is no set answer for the ideal number of individuals on a council. Larry Osborne suggests 12 members to be the maximum size.[1] Many councils that are larger function effectively because chairs of major committees serve on the council and can make their reports as part of the council meeting.

Term Limits

Religious organizations differ as to whether to include term limits for council members or officers. Unfortunately, many organizations use term limits rather than taking other steps to remove council members who are not functioning.

The case against term limits is made by the dean of nonprofit lawyers, Donald Kramer. Kramer's article on this topic is entitled "Term Limits Are For Cowards: Arbitrary End of Service Assures That Organizations Lose Some of Their Best Talent."[2] As Kramer states: "We think the primary reason most people like term limits is so that they don't have to ask 'dead wood' directors to leave the Board. It gives them a convenient way to let them go without risking confrontation."[3]

Church councils should institute numerous procedures for ensuring that every council member is excellent. First, the by-laws should provide for the automatic removal of any council member not attending meetings. A common provision is that an individual who misses three consecutive council meetings without an excuse is automatically removed. Members who do not meet other council responsibilities such as serving on a committee or making a financial contribution to the church should be contacted by a member of the council development committee and reminded of their obligations. If they refuse to meet these obligations, they should be asked to resign.

Another effective method is to have fixed terms for council members. Council members should have a job description. Well before the elections, the council development committee should meet to review the record of each council member:

- Meeting attendance.
- Financial contribution.
- Sitting on one active committee.

Council members who do not attend meetings or meet the other requirements for council membership should not be re-nominated. Another reason given for term limits is that individuals with new ideas can join the council. See if there are other ways to get new blood. What have general turnover rates been in the last several years? Have council members resigned because they moved out of the community or no longer wished to meet their council responsibilities?

Larry Osborne, in his book *Sticky Teams,* also argues for short terms and no term limits for council members. He suggests one-year terms that can be renewed indefinitely. As he says, "We have some board members who've served over twenty years. They've not grown stagnant. They've grown wise."[4] You can also get new council members by permitting the council chair to appoint a number of council members at any time, or to expand the number of council members at any time.

The same argument holds for not having term limits for officers. A council chair who is doing an excellent job should be re-elected. Once a council finds a secretary who takes excellent minutes and distributes them to the council in a timely fashion, this individual should continue to be re-elected.

One alternative is the "modified term limit" for council members and officers. The by-laws state that though there are term limits, the council can waive the provision for specific council members or officers.

Past Chairs

Many councils find that it is important to take advantage of the experience of past council chairs. Some include the immediate past chair as a voting council member. Other councils include all past chairs as board members. Some include all past chairs as voting members and others include all past chairs as nonvoting members.

Salaries and Benefits

Salaries and benefits for all staff members should be approved by the church council. Before salaries are approved, the personnel committee should make a recommendation to the council. It is recommended that salaries for all staff members be reviewed once a year. This effort should be coordinated with the finance committee so that enough funds are included in the budget to pay salaries and fringe benefits of all employees. All employees should receive written notification of the health insurance and other benefits they receive. This statement should also include the number of vacation and sick days the individual is entitled to during the year. State whether the leave must be taken in that year or whether any leave can be carried over to a succeeding year.

Disciplinary Procedures

Councils of religious organizations find it helpful to include written disciplinary procedures for the staff in their by-laws. These include a list of which offenses require immediate suspension and which require a warning. Then, if there is inappropriate conduct, the council can just refer to the personnel policies for the penalties.

Officers

Most religious organizations function like other nonprofit organizations. The council chair is a volunteer and leads the meetings. Other duties of the chair should be spelled out in writing, such as appointing committee chairs. The minister attends all council meetings, but is not a member of the council.

Most religious organizations find that a one-year term is too short. Many elect their officers to two-year terms. Think through the role of the vice-chair or several vice-chairs carefully. It certainly is traditional to have the vice-chair act in the absence of the chair. But it is important to give the vice-chairs specific duties in addition. In organizations with numerous committees, for example, it is helpful for each vice-chair to serve as council liaison for a number of committees. In many organizations, the first vice-chair is expected to assume the chair's position at the end of the chair's term in office.

Revisions to By-Laws

Many organizations make it much too difficult to change by-laws. The council should be able to revise the by-laws. It should not be necessary to wait an entire year for by-law revisions. One requirement should be that by-law changes should be reviewed by the by-laws committee and the recommendation of the by-laws committee should be sent to the council. The only other requirement should be adequate notice. Certainly, the recommendation of the by-laws committee should be in writing and submitted to the council in writing before the meeting. Some groups require a three-quarters vote of the council to approve by-law changes.

Annual Congregational Meeting

Many churches have an annual congregational meeting. The "business" of the church is conducted by the council. However, the congregational meeting can have many other purposes:

- The council chair informs the congregation of the major events that have taken place during the past year.
- The council chair informs the congregation of major events planned for the upcoming year.
- The minister outlines upcoming religious services and holidays, and gives an uplifting spiritual message to the congregation.
- A written report of the activities of each committee should be distributed to those in attendance.
- All congregants should be encouraged to sign up for at least one standing committee.
- The treasurer should submit a financial report to the congregation. The written report as well as any major changes from previous reports should be discussed with the congregation.

Dates the Church Office Is Open

List in the by-laws the specific hours the church office is open and the holidays when it is closed. Indicate the procedures for determining whether religious services or other church activities will be cancelled for inclement weather.

Forming Active Committees

One major difference between a well-run church and just an average one is the way committees are run. A significant part of each council meeting should include discussion of the recommendations of each committee. Begin by thinking about which committees are needed. One effective way to do this is to write a single page about each committee, including the following information:

- Name of committee.
- Name, phone number, e-mail address of chair.
- Examples of assignments.
- How often committee meets (monthly, quarterly, as needed).
- Where the committee meets (church, restaurant, home).
- Staff assigned to committee (minister, executive director, educational director).
- To whom the committee chair reports (council chair, council vice chair, minister, executive director).

In most organizations, the council chair appoints the chair of each committee. The committee chair is told the expectations of the council chair in certain areas:

- How often the committee will meet.
- The responsibilities of the committee.
- Whether the committee chair is responsible for selecting committee members.

- Which church staff member is assigned to assist the committee.
- Deadlines for committee reports.

Selecting Committee Members

When the committee chair selects committee members, several techniques can be used:

- All church members are eligible to serve on all committees.
- The chair should meet with potential committee members to ask them to serve. Personal meetings are more effective than phone calls or e-mails.
- The chair may send e-mails to a large number of individuals to invite them to attend the first committee meeting.
- At each meeting, the date, time, and location of the next meeting are set.
- For small committees, the date of each committee meeting is set in advance to help ensure 100-percent attendance.
- An e-mail is sent to remind individuals to attend the next meeting and to recommend others for committee membership.

The minutes of each committee meeting should be in writing. They should include committee attendance and decisions. The minutes also should include specific assignments with deadlines. It is also extremely helpful to include any motions that are to be made to the church council.

All committees are advisory except when the council gives a committee specific approval to act on its own. For the committee to take official action requires council approval.

Most committee meetings are open to all church members. Listing all committee meetings in the church bulletin and inviting church members to attend will emphasize that the church "belongs to everyone." All church members should be requested to serve on at least one committee.

In some churches, all council members are required to chair or co-chair a committee. In others, all council members are required to participate on a standing committee. An effective technique is for the council chair to appoint ad hoc committees. When there are particular issues that would benefit from a discussion by a small group, the chair appoints such a group and gives the members a specific assignment and a timetable to report back to the council.

One way to predict who would make an excellent council member is to see who has been active on committees. An individual who has attended all the meetings of the worship committee, for example, would be a good candidate for council membership.

In many churches, the officers serve as the executive committee. Many churches find having an active executive committee is effective. It provides a place to discuss problems that arise between meetings and to develop strategies for solving them. In some churches, a role of the executive committee is to prepare the agenda for the next council meeting. In other churches, the chair automatically heads the executive committee and appoints its members. In this way, individuals who have earned the respect of the congregation can play a major role in the decision-making process.

Some churches state in their by-laws that the executive committee has the power to act on behalf of the council between meetings. If the executive committee has this power, it should be careful not to abuse it. For example, if the executive committee takes formal action, members of the council should be notified in writing of the actions of the executive committee.

Here is a list of some common standing committees:

- Adult Education.
- Audit.
- Budget.
- Building.
- By-laws.
- Catering.
- Cemetery.
- Community Outreach.

- Council Development.
- Education.
- Endowment.
- Executive.
- Finance.
- Fundraising.
- Life-Cycle Events.
- Membership.
- Minister Liaison.
- Personnel.
- Planning.
- Property.
- Religious Leader Search.
- Social Ministry.
- Worship.
- Volunteers.
- Youth Education.

It is recommended that every church activity and special event have its own planning committee. To as great an extent as possible, events should be planned by the participants. For example, events for singles should be planned by singles; senior citizens programs should be planned by seniors.

Committee Meetings

All committee meetings should begin with the distribution of a written agenda by the chair. The committee should review the agenda to see if everyone agrees on the tasks to be accomplished at the meeting.

The meeting procedures should be informal. There should be no votes and no Robert's Rules of Order. The chair should encourage full discussion by all attendees.

If possible, a staff member should be present at each committee meeting. That individual can be given assignments by the group such as researching information on a topic and bringing it to the next committee meeting.

Either the staff member, the committee chair, or another member should agree to take minutes. When it seems there is consensus on an issue, be sure the chair states the consensus clearly for the minutes. The minutes should include only:

- Name of committee.

- Attendance.

- Unanimous conclusions of committee.

- Minority views if committee wishes to include them.

- Motions to be made to church council.

Each committee meeting should end with setting the date for the next committee meeting. Try to pick a date when all committee members can attend. Remind the members that if they cannot attend any committee meeting, they should let the chair know in advance.

8

Personnel Policies

Every workplace should have written personnel policies, and churches are no exception. Personnel policies should be detailed so that confusion and misunderstanding are avoided. Here are some of the common sections of church personnel policies.

Holidays and Inclement Weather

List the days the church office is closed. Remember to include both national and religious holidays. Decide in advance if the church office is closed the day after Thanksgiving and the day before Christmas. If a national holiday falls on the weekend, is the church closed on the Friday preceding it or Monday after it?

Who decides if the church is closed during inclement weather? What is the system for congregants learning whether the church is closed, and therefore services are cancelled?

Work Schedule

Have specific work schedule policies for all employees. Be sure to have a special policy for the minister. Remember that if services are held on Sunday, the minister is "working" that day. It is appropriate to give all employees two days off each week. It is, of course, understood the minister is "on call" to deal with emergencies. Try not to "burn out" the minister. Be sure he/she takes time off during each week.

Pay Procedures and Salary Increases

Do employees receive a pay check once a month, twice a month, or every other week? What are the procedures for employees receiving salary increases? Are salaries set by the council? Are there automatic increases for particular lengths of service?

Vacations, Sabbaticals, Resignations, and Sick Leave

How many vacation days does each employee earn? What is the policy for accumulating vacation days? Must the vacation days be taken in the year they are earned or can they be carried over? Are there special vacation rules for the minister?

Many religious leaders receive a sabbatical after a number of years of service. If so, spell out the terms. List whether the minister receives a partial salary during the sabbatical period.

How many weeks' notice must employees give if they resign?

It should be clear that employees should not work if they are sick. Policies for the number of days they get paid if they are sick should be included in the personnel policies.

Benefits

Do employees receive healthcare benefits? If so, are family members of the employee covered? Does the employee pay part of the monthly or quarterly healthcare fees? Is there a pension fund? If so, what are the payment arrangements?

Special Benefits for the Minister

Many congregations have special rules for the minister. Which national ministerial conferences can the minister attend? Are all expenses paid for by the congregation?

Some special benefits may relate to the minister's home. Spell them out clearly. If the minister lives in a house owned by the church, what are the procedures for making repairs? Who shovels the snow?

Performance Evaluations

Note the policy. Many churches evaluate new employees after they have worked for three months. Annual performance reviews are common. (Refer to Chapter 3 of this book for further information.)

Probationary Periods

Include a probationary period for all employees. During this period, employees can be terminated without notice or a hearing. After this period, the employee's rights on termination should be spelled out, including rules for hearings and notice.

Grievance Procedures

Formal procedures for filing grievances should be included in the personnel policies. As with other organizations, all employee grievances should be submitted in writing to his/her supervisor. The supervisor must be required to reply to the grievance in writing within a set period of time. The employee should then have the right to appeal the decision of the supervisor to the personnel committee. In most churches, the personnel committee has the final decision on the matter.

Criminal Charges

Specific rules should be included if a church employee is accused of a crime or convicted of a crime. For example, the personnel committee could recommend that an employee who is accused or convicted of specific offenses be put on leave with pay, leave without pay, or terminated. Procedures should be outlined for notifying law enforcement authorities of possible violations of criminal laws.

Severance Pay

If an employee is terminated by the church, what are the rules for severance pay and unused vacation time?

9

Fundraising

Religious organizations raise funds in various ways. Some pass around a plate at religious services asking congregants to make contributions. Some charge dues to be a "member" of the congregation. Most churches ask their members for donations. Many have special events such as fairs, food events, and lectures. Several rent out the church hall to members and to the general community for weddings, birthdays, and other special occasions.

It is important that council members are aware of the net receipts of fundraising efforts and devise ways to increase them. What is important is that the church has funds in the bank to meet the needs of the congregation.

As with other aspects of church life, begin by appointing a fundraising committee. Appoint individuals to this committee who have expertise in fundraising. Be sure to include individuals with the financial ability to make large donations to the church and to ask their friends to make similar donations.

The fundraising committee has the responsibility of developing an annual fundraising plan for the church. One excellent resource in developing and implementing the plan is *Ask and You Shall Receive: A Fundraising Training Program for Religious Organizations and Projects*. Kim Klein gives the good news that the long tradition of giving to religious organizations makes fundraising for churches easier than for nonprofits in general.[1] More than half of the funds given by United States citizens are given to religious organizations.[2]

The fundraising committee should start the process by outlining all the receipts by the church for the past several years. Then calculate the net "profits" for each special event. If the church had a raffle, for example, receipts are listed as one line under "Receipts-Raffle." Be sure, however, that "Expenditures-Raffle" has several lines, including prizes, postage, printing tickets, and dinner costs. There should also be a "Net Profits-Raffle" line, which would be "Receipts-Raffle" less "Expenditures-Raffle."

Increasing Receipts

The fundraising committee should review every net profit line from the past three years to see how net profits can be increased. Churches that pass around a collection plate should consider ways of increasing revenues. A direct method is to ask congregants for increased contributions. It is appropriate for the minister to request increased contributions as part of the Sunday service. Remember, however, that not all members attend services. Periodic letters from the council chair and announcements in the church bulletin and on the church Website encouraging increased contributions to the church are helpful.

In order to encourage increased contributions, each church should assist congregants in following Internal Revenue Service rules so that their contributions are tax deductible. For example, the Pension Protection Act of 2006 prohibits donors from deducting contributions to churches unless they can produce records of the transactions. All churches should therefore provide congregants with an envelope with the donor's name or identifying number on it. The church bookkeeper then provides congregants with an end-of-the-year statement with a total of the donations. Other rules permit individuals 70 and a half years or older to contribute up to $100,000 from an IRA directly to a church without penalty.

The fundraising committee should develop an annual fundraising plan. It might include visiting congregants to ask for donations to the church. As with any type of fundraising, visiting individuals in their homes to ask for donations is far more successful than calling or writing letters. Individuals may be asked for special donations as church sponsors or patrons. Churches may also have telephone or letter-writing campaigns to ask for contributions.

Asking for donations for a specific project or to purchase a specific item for the church is always more successful than asking for a general donation to help balance the church's budget. If the item is expensive, requesting that a number of individuals give small pledges is a worthwhile technique. Putting a plaque on the wall next to the item such as a new church organ that lists the name of the donors often leads to more successful fundraising.

Fundraising Dinners

Many churches raise significant sums of money by holding dinners for special occasions. It is important to select an honoree or honorees celebrating a special occasion. Examples of such occasions might include:

- 25th anniversary of the minister serving the church.
- 50th anniversary of the ordination of the minister.
- 50th wedding anniversary of strong church supporters.
- 10th year the council chair has served in that role.
- Honoring the church's confirmation class.
- A congregant winning a special community award.
- Congregants celebrating 90th, 95th, or 100th birthdays.
- Milestone anniversary of the church (honoring present and former ministers and council chairs) every 25 years.

Begin by establishing a dinner committee. Be sure it includes relatives and special friends of the honoree as well as well-respected church members. Select a dinner committee chair who:

- Is well-respected by the congregation.
- Is a longtime friend of the honoree.
- Will make a large lead gift.

The honoree is asked to give the dinner committee a long list of relatives, friends, and business associates. The list should have complete mailing addresses, because the invitation will be sent by mail. It also should include as many e-mail addresses as possible for follow-up mailings.

Patrons and Sponsors

Send letters under the signature of the dinner committee chair to a list of potential dinner patrons and sponsors. A small "patrons and sponsors subcommittee" might be established to decide who should receive these letters. The subcommittee might include the honoree and a small number of church members. Letters should be sent to:

- Wealthy church members.
- Family members of the honoree.
- Friends of the honoree outside the church.

Send the information about the event along with the mimimum amount of the contribution to be listed in the program book as a patron or sponsor. Note that patrons and sponsors will receive two complimentary tickets to the dinner.

Ask the recipients of this letter to fill out a form indicating if they will agree to be patrons or sponsors and return it with a check by the due date. The amounts will be set by the dinner committee. Because the contributors are getting two "free" tickets, a good rule of thumb is that the donation for sponsors is 10 times the single ticket price and the donation for patrons is five times the single ticket price. (If a dinner ticket is $60, the sponsor cost is $600 and the patron cost is $300.)

Complimentary Tickets

Mail complimentary tickets for the dinner to:

- The honoree.
- The honoree's immediate family.
- Staff of the church who might have financial difficulties purchasing tickets.
- Friends or relatives of the honoree who might have financial difficulties purchasing tickets.

Location

If the church has a social hall large enough to accommodate all of the guests, the dinner should be held in the church. Be sure, however, that the church is specially decorated for the occasion. A decorations subcommittee should decorate the church with table centerpieces, balloons, streamers, or anything that will make it look festive. It may be appropriate for the church to rent items such as tablecloths, cloth napkins, and comfortable chairs.

Dinner Invitation

A dinner invitation should be sent to each invitee that:

- Notes the honoree.
- Includes a current picture of the honoree and a brief description of that individual's accomplishments.
- Lists the special church programs that will be supported by donations from the dinner.
- Indicates the amount of each dinner ticket, how the check should be made out, and the address of the church.
- States that individuals who cannot attend the dinner are invited to make a contribution to the church in the name of the honoree.
- Lists the event sponsors and patrons.
- Asks how the names of the donors should be listed on the donor list to be published in the program book and the church bulletin.

Donations Subcommittee

A donations subcommittee should have the goal of having all the dinner costs covered. Ask businesses such as printers not to charge for their services. Ask congregational donors to cover costs such as food, drinks, and servers.

Program Book Ads

A program book subcommittee should be responsible for obtaining advertisements. The request for ads should include the cost of each ad size and the deadline for submitting print-ready text. Businesses that should be solicited include:

- Every company from which the church purchases goods and services (office supplies, religious supplies, funeral homes, florists, printers).
- All businesses within a mile of the church.
- Major business with whom the congregants do business (banks, restaurants, supermarkets).
- Businesses with a connection to the honoree, including the employer of the honoree and business associates.

If possible, requests to place ads in the ad book should be made in person. The ads can be sent to the church. Confirmation of dinner reservations might include the opportunity to place a congratulatory note in the program book.

Program Book

All attendees receive a program book when they arrive at the dinner. The program book includes the following:

- Dinner program.
- Picture and bio of the honoree.
- Description of major church programs.
- List of dinner sponsors and patrons.
- List of dinner committee and subcommittee chairs and members.
- Ads.

Program

The following is a basic framework for the dinner:

- The church council chair welcomes everyone.
- The dinner committee chair welcomes everyone and introduces any special guests, such as relatives of the honoree, political leaders, friends of the honoree who have traveled long distances to attend, and dignitaries from other churches.
- The church choir or a soloist or musician offers a musical number.
- The minister delivers an opening prayer.
- Dinner is served (except for dessert).
- The dinner chair welcomes the honoree and stresses the particular church programs the honoree has supported.
- The honoree makes a short speech welcoming everyone and encouraging support for the church.
- The dinner committee chair thanks the honoree and lists special programs at the church that could be expanded if additional funds were raised. Programs for youth and the elderly are often emphasized.

- The dinner committee chair notes that on the table are pledge cards. He/she asks the attendees to check a pledge fund block and give the pledge card to an usher.
- During the interlude, while the pledge cards are being collected, there is another musical number.
- Dessert is served.
- The minister gives the closing benediction.
- The council chair adjourns the dinner.

Food and Service

The quality of the food and the service should be excellent. In some congregations, the meal can be prepared and served by congregants. Do not sacrifice the quality of the food and service to save money, however.

After the Dinner

After the dinner, a letter under the signature of the dinner chair is sent to those who made pledges. It lists the amount of the pledge, to whom the check should be made out, and the name and address of the church. Note which part of the contribution is deductible for federal income tax purposes. Thank the donor.

A letter under the signature of the dinner chair is sent to everyone who did not attend the dinner. It describes how wonderful the event was and how much has already been raised. The letter points to specific church programs that could be expanded if additional funds are raised. It includes a picture of the honoree at the dinner shaking hands with a visiting dignitary (the mayor, the bishop). The letter includes a request for donations, states how checks should be made out, and includes the address of the church.

Wills and Bequests

Every church should have a wills and bequests program as a major ongoing fundraiser. First, set up a wills and bequests committee. Include on it several attorneys and financial advisors.

A brochure should be prepared that provides information about financial reasons for having wills. Congregants who have wills should be encouraged to change their wills to include a bequest to the church. Most churches can find attorneys willing to change existing wills at no cost if the only change is to make a bequest to the church. Perhaps a group of attorneys would agree to provide wills for congregants at a low fixed fee.

Individuals should be encouraged to memorialize their loved ones by purchasing several lines on a memorial plaque. Special memorial funds can be established in memory of beloved congregants. The closer the fund is established to the time of death of the congregant, the more money will be raised. One effective technique is for the chair of the wills and bequests committee, upon hearing of the death of a prominent congregant or of a former or present staff member, to contact the next of kin. Similarly, each church should have memorial plaques.

After offering sincere condolences, the chair should ask the next of kin for permission to establish a memorial fund at the church. The next of kin should be asked to place a line in the obituary in the local newspaper requesting individuals to make donations to the memorial fund at the church.

The church office should send out a notice in a black border to all congregants noting the death and announcing the establishment of the memorial fund. An attempt should be made to earmark the proceeds of the fund to a cause the deceased supported, perhaps programs for youth.

Upon receiving the donation, the contributor should be sent a thank-you note from the church that lists the amount of the donation. The next of kin is notified of the gift (without listing the amount of the gift). The note to the next of kin includes the name and address of the donor. Every church should encourage all of its members when placing an obituary for any loved one in the local newspaper to request that donations be made to the church in memory of the deceased. In addition, church members should be encouraged to make donations to the church in memory of any individual.

Stewardship

Every church should have a well-planned comprehensive appeal or series of appeals for regular contributions to the church. Churches have numerous names for this effort. Many churches request their members to tithe, or pledge a percentage of their income to the church.

Many churches call the campaign a "stewardship" program. An excellent Model for Congregational Stewardship is included in Appendix 5. Some churches stress contibutions to the church's endowment fund. When a church establishes an endowment fund, the principal is invested. The interest may be used for regular or special church expenditures. Other churches encourage planned giving, including annuities, giving appreciated stocks, and charitable life insurance.

Other Fundraising Events

Many churches have a series of plaques to note special celebratory events such as birthdays, anniversaries, weddings, or major job appointments. Congregants are urged to make contributions to the church to note any happy occasion.

Church dinners or fairs are common fundraising events. Many churches raise funds from silent or live auctions. Church raffles are very common. Council members must review the profits made on each special event. All too often, a church runs an event that loses money each year and yet it continues to run that event.

The key to the success of nearly every church fundraising event is the number and quality of volunteers. See Chapter 15 of this book for tips on getting and keeping volunteers. Every event should have its own subcommittee and group of volunteers. It is important to identify specific volunteers and tasks before announcing the special event. Having more volunteers and reducing the time commitment for each volunteer is a good strategy.

Be sure to contact other churches to learn about their experiences with special events. In many cases, copying their materials, with their permission, can save time and money. Avoiding problems other groups have experienced is always worthwhile.

Lyle E. Schaller, in *44 Questions for Congregational Self-Appraisal,* states that an increasing number of congregations depend on 10 to 15 income streams:

- Offering plate.
- User fees.

- Memorials.
- Bequests.
- Large gifts.
- Income from investments.
- Sales.
- Small appeal.
- Big appeal.
- Three year capital funds appeal.
- Rentals.
- Outsiders.
- Foundations and corporations.
- Governments.
- Money-raising events.
- Denominational subsidies.[3]

The secret of church fundraising is to plan, plan, plan. Having a successful fundraising committee for each event will prove to be a successful strategy.

10

Fiscal Procedures and Cutting Expenditures

A church is responsible to God for stressing the highest level of morality. Certainly in its fiscal procedures it should reflect these high moral standards.

First, it is essential for every church to have a detailed budget. Start by forming a finance committee. The chair of the finance committee should be a council member. In some churches, the council treasurer automatically chairs the finance committee. Several members of the finance committee should have fiscal experience, either in their "day job" or other volunteer positions.

Begin the process by preparing a list of all receipts and expenditures for the preceding year in as much detail as possible. The finance committee then reviews every budget line for the preceding year and makes predictions as to whether the line will increase, decrease, or remain the same for the next year.

In many instances, the finance committee must consult with other committees. For example, the finance committee must obtain figures from the personnel committee on the salaries and fringe benefits to include in the budget. It must get estimates from the fundraising committee about estimated receipts and expenditures for special events.

Before the fiscal year begins, the finance committee presents the proposed budget to the church council. The council makes changes and approves the budget. At each subsequent council meeting, the finance committee chair submits 1) the budget previously approved by the council, 2) the receipts and expenditures to date, and 3) a narrative of why major items are higher or lower than expected. No church official is authorized to make an expenditure unless 1) the item was included in the budget approved by the council, or 2) the council gives special permission to make that expenditure. Appendix 9 gives questions every church should ask itself about its fiscal procedures, and Appendix 10 offers an extensive list of receipts and expenditures common to most churches.

Special Events

It is extremely important to set up an accounting system to keep track of all receipts and expenditures relating to any special event. That way, the council can determine if this is an event that made a profit and exactly what that profit was.

When receiving a check made out to the church, the church bookkeeper must be clear to which fund the money should be allocated. For example, if a check is for tickets for the annual church fundraising dinner, the total must be allocated to that account. In fact, all expenditures for the annual church fundraising dinner should be allocated to that account. The costs for stamps for the solicitation mailing should be charged to that account as well as the amount paid to the kitchen help for the dinner. The cost of the food for the dinner should be charged to the dinner account. When the treasurer makes his/her report to the council, the net amount of the dinner (receipts less expenditures) should be reported.

Written Fiscal Policies

The church should have written fiscal policies and follow those policies. No check should be signed if that expenditure does not appear in the budget. Items costing more than a certain amount should not be authorized unless written bids are obtained.

Who can sign checks? It is prudent to have two signatures on every check. A check should not be signed unless a bill or other authorization is attached. Very little cash should be kept in the church. Individuals authorized to take a small amount from petty cash should fill out a slip that includes their name, date, amount, and the reason for the withdrawal. The total of the amount in the petty cash box and the total of the slips should never vary.

Cutting Expenditures

Too many churches pay attention to increasing church revenues while devoting too little time to reducing church expenditures.
If significant efforts to reduce costs are made, churches often find
that it is easier to reduce costs than to increase receipts. Begin the
process by listing every expenditure in detail for the past calendar
year. Then the finance committee should review expenditures to see
which ones can be reduced. A number of methods should be used
to determine which services can be provided at substantially lower
rates. Ask church members who are businesspeople to either provide the church with complimentary services or offer the services at
a reduced rate.

For example, many churches are still paying outside vendors
to print and mail the church bulletin. Begin by seeing whether the
bulletin can be printed on the church computer. In some instances,
a parishioner may have the skills to print it. In other instances, a
church staff member can obtain appropriate computer training.
Many churches are beginning to send their bulletin on-line rather
then by mailing. Many other forms of church correspondence can
be sent by e-mail. Remember, however, that not all church members
have e-mail, so be sure members without e-mail receive information
by U.S. mail. Some congregations ask congregants whether they wish
to receive the church bulletin online or by mail.

One technique to lower expenditures is to require several written bids for major projects. If the church needs a new roof, for example, obtain several bids. Make certain each vendor submits references
along with their bids. If the church is being renovated, it is important to visit several churches the bidder has renovated. If the church
needs a new roof, be sure an expert in roofing reviews each bid.

Ask vendors for discounts on bulk purchases. Rather than paying retail prices for office supplies, for example, money can be saved
by estimating the quantity of supplies needed in a year and asking
several office supply companies to offer discounts if the church buys
only from them. Another technique is to join with several churches
and to ask for discounts if they all buy from the same vendor.

Think through which expenditures can be reduced. Having all
baked goods prepared by volunteers can save significant sums. Asking

volunteers to serve the food at church dinners saves money, because the expenditures for outside help will be significantly reduced.

Just knowing how much items cost can reduce expenditures. When you know the total costs of having a wedding at the church, for example, the banquet committee can make an informed decision of how much to charge a family for a church wedding. Many churches have different prices for weddings and other events, depending on the particular menu and the services selected. A congregant will be charged extra, for example, if the youth group mans the cloak room or the church provides valet parking services.

Once the costs are known for each event, the decision of what to charge can be made. Should the church have one price for church members and another for non-members? Does the church want to break even on the fee charged to church members or does it want to make a profit?

Review every expenditure, including monthly bills. Do different phone calling plans charge varied amounts? Can the church save money on electricity by revising the billing plan?

Many churches can lower expenditures by sending "wish lists" to their members. Members are told how much specific items cost and are asked to make a contribution. If new prayer books are needed because some are in disrepair, there is no need for the church to pay for the new ones. Congregants can be asked to make donations to a Prayer Book Fund. The church will put a dedication page noting the book is dedicated in memory or in honor of individuals designated by the congregant.

11

Capital Campaigns

One challenge faced by every religious organization is how to raise funds to build a new church or to remodel an existing one. A project of this significance needs to be thoroughly planned and carried out to ensure its success.

Considering Building Options

Begin by carefully studying the future needs of the church. If a decision is made to refurbish the church, the newly remodeled church must meet the needs not only of the congregation of today, but the congregation of the next 25 years. Here is where the strategic planning committee (Chapter 13) is charged with estimating future needs. Will the need for classrooms be increasing or decreasing during the next 25 years? The need for more pews? More office space? Are all parts of the church handicapped-accessible?

Get ideas of a range of costs. A totally different plan is an order if you are raising $100,000 than if you must raise several million dollars. It is important, therefore, to have estimates of the cost for renovations to the existing church or building a new one. If you are constructing a new facility, you may want estimates of the costs of a smaller, simpler building and a larger, more elaborate one.

The council's building and grounds committee should begin by studying whether and when repairs are needed and developing a report for the council. The committee should begin the discussion of the future needs of the church. Interviews with the minister and the church principal should be an essential part in the development of this report.

How Much Will It Cost?

Try to get a ballpark idea of how much it would cost the church to either renovate the existing space or build a new church or a church extension. In many cases, an architect will give you estimates at no cost. Architects do this because they would like favorable consideration if you decide to go ahead with the building effort. In other cases, you will have to pay a small sum for these estimates.

When considering several options, remember to include:

- A factor for estimated inflation.
- Estimated interest charges to borrow funds until future pledges are paid.
- The costs of any consultants you retain.

How Much Can You Raise?

An essential piece of the puzzle is to estimate how much money can be raised from congregant donations. Though there may be other fundraising opportunities, a large percentage of the funds raised will most likely come from church members. In addition, you will find that more than half of the funds raised in any capital campaign will be contributed by 10 percent of the donors.

There are many ways of estimating how much can be raised from church members. One effective method is to establish a small committee of church leaders to visit some of the wealthier congregants and ask for their input. Do they think this is a good time to raise funds? Do they have any ideas for fundraising procedures? Approximately how much would they pledge?

Campaign Consultant

Another way to proceed is to retain a capital campaign consultant. Most churches find that they do not have the expertise to run a capital campaign without a consultant. Begin by asking three firms that have experience in consulting on capital campaigns to submit written bids. The bids must include:

- Three churches they can give as references.
- The name, address, phone number, and e-mail address of the chair of the campaign committee in these three churches.

- Specific consultant duties.
- Payment amounts and schedules.
- Cancellation clause for both parties.

Then contact the chair of the campaign committee in each of the three congregations and ask them questions about the services they received from the consulting firm. Ask each representative specific questions:

- How many members does the church have?
- How much was raised?
- What was the period of time for the campaign?
- What were the strengths of the consultant?
- What were the weaknesses of the consultant?
- If they had another capital campaign, would they hire the same consultant?

Interview representatives of several consulting firms in person. Make certain to meet with the specific individuals who would be assigned to your church if the contract were awarded. Discuss with the campaign consultant the options of conducting a feasibility study. Often the consultant interviews several congregants and then submits a report giving estimates of how much might be raised in a capital campaign.

If the capital campaign committee decides to ask the consultant to conduct the feasibility study, meet with the individual at the consulting firm who would be doing the interviewing. Discuss the questions he/she would be asking. In many cases, the individuals being interviewed will be asked if they want the information they provide to be confidential. Individuals with major complaints about the church, for example, will not want their names revealed. In most instances, however, the church member will be happy to have the interviewer share the information they provide with the capital campaign committee or the council.

Whether to Raise Funds

In most churches, the church council is the body that makes the decision about whether to go ahead with the capital campaign. The council should begin by reviewing two reports. One report outlines the need for the refurbishment of the existing structure or for a new church. The other is a report on the potential of the church members for contributing the needed funds. Get input from the minister and the rest of the church staff as well.

Also, obtain input from other churches about the amounts they raised for capital campaigns. Often, a national church office or a judicatory compiles information about the experiences of churches in other parts of the country. Another church in your community of a similar size may have recently completed a capital campaign, and the campaign chair may be willing to share experiences with you.

Be certain before coming to a final decision that all council members understand that they:

- Must make a pledge to the campaign.
- Must encourage fellow congregants to make a pledge to the campaign.
- Must be extremely patient, as building or refurbishing is a long and stressful process.
- Will be called on as church leaders to volunteer to help in the fundraising process.

Remember: Do not proceed unless you are sure of succeeding. You must have:

- An estimate of the costs you will incur.
- A feasibility study that indicates you can raise the sum required.
- The commitment of every council member to make a pledge and to support the campaign.

If these elements do not exist, consider postponing the campaign until you do have them.

When You Are Ready to Begin

After the council takes a formal vote to undertake a building campaign, the council chair should appoint the capital campaign committee chair and the building committee chair.

These are individuals who should:

- Be well-respected by all congregants.
- Have demonstrated leadership qualities.

- Have the ability to make the necessary time commitment.
- Have participated in similar major community projects.
- Be willing to make a major campaign pledge.

The campaign committee chair and the building committee chair are assisted by the council chair, the minister, and perhaps other board members to recommend the appointment of the members of both committees.

Each member of the campaign committee and the building committee must agree to:

- Serve as the chair of a campaign subcommittee.
- Attend every meeting of the campaign committee.
- Make a pledge to the campaign.

Discuss the commitment of the paid staff to the capital campaign. The minister, school principal, secretary, financial manager, and other paid staff must be willing and able to devote significant amounts of time to the capital campaign.

Building Committee

The building committee is essential to the success of the project. Include:

- Individuals with building expertise (architects, builders).
- At least one representative of the staff, for example school principal.
- Several board members.
- Potential large donors.

The building committee would begin the process by discussing the types of rooms required in the new or refurbished building, such as:

- Main sanctuary.
- Chapel.
- Classrooms.

- Social hall.
- Kitchen.
- Offices.
- Restrooms.
- Gymnasium.
- Lobby.

Try to be as specific as possible as to the needs of the church of the future. For example, be sure to consider the parking lot carefully, a constant problem to many churches cramped for outdoor space. It is necessary to have a place to park cars that is easily accessible to the church facility, and this may require purchasing an adjoining property. Be certain that all aspects of the building—the sanctuary, the rest rooms, the offices—are fully handicapped accessible. All churches have a moral (if not a legal) obligation to meet the needs of the disabled.

Campaign Subcommittees

The campaign committee chair appoints the heads of the campaign subcommittees. These should include the following:

- Large gifts.
- Medium and small gifts.
- Publicity.
- Events.
- Financial.
- Dedication opportunities.

The chair of the building committee should be invited to meetings of the campaign committee; the chair of the campaign committee should be invited to several meetings of the building committee.

Dedication Opportunities

Many churches find that substantial sums can be raised through dedication opportunities. Be clear about the amount of the pledge needed for each dedication opportunity. Pledges can be made in memory or in honor of a loved one; they can be made in the name of the company making a contribution. Dedication opportunities could include:

- Name of a room.
- Name on a memory plaque. This may include the name of the deceased and the donor.
- Name on an honoring plaque. This may include the name(s) of the individuals being honored, the occasion (for example, 50th wedding anniversary), and the donor.

For smaller gifts, provide other opportunities. Many churches have permanent bricks with the names of donors; others may have a plaque or a book in the lobby of the church with the names of donors.

Selecting an Architect

Once the campaign committee has identified potential architects, arrange a visit by the building committee chair to a church that has recently been built or refurbished by each architect. Take a detailed tour of the building. Get as much information as you can from representatives of the church you are visiting. Ask specific questions about positive and negative experiences with the architect.

Preparing a Campaign Brochure

Spend time developing a campaign brochure that includes:

- Reasons for the new building or church expansion.
- Architect's drawing of the new building.
- Dedication opportunities.

Be sure the brochure is easy to read and attractive. It should include details on how to make out a donation check and the mailing address of the church.

The brochure will be used for all parts of the campaign. Give it to all individuals whom you visit to ask for a pledge. Include it in every mail solicitation and in every packet given out at each meeting that discusses the campaign. Place it in every church pew.

Visiting Potentially Large Donors

It is clear from reviewing the results of successful church capital campaigns that, by far, the lion's share of funds is pledged by members who are visited in their homes by other church members. Begin by calling a meeting of the large gifts subcommittee. In all cases, the members should be respected members of the congregation. In most cases, they begin by making large pledges themselves. The large gifts subcommittee then proceeds by:

- Making a list of families to visit. These are individuals the committee members consider are financially able to make major contributions to the campaign.
- Making a call to set up an appointment when all the adult members of the family will be present.
- Sometimes, one member of the committee visits; at other times, two members do. Ideally, any visitors should be personal friends of the family being visited. Churches have different policies or traditions about whether the minister serves as a member of the large gifts committee and visits congregants in their homes.

Telephone Calls

Members of the medium and small gifts subcommittee should call every congregant on the phone who will not be visited in person. Try to arrange the phone calls so that each individual receives a call from a friend. Send these individuals the capital campaign brochure by mail. This will include a drawing of what the church will look like and the campaign's final financial goal. Tell them they will receive a phone call from a volunteer on the capital campaign committee.

Begin the phone call by asking if the individual has received the capital campaign brochure. Ask the individual to talk about his/her involvement in the church. Do not interrupt. After the individual has spoken for a while, ask for a generous pledge. Note how many years the individual will be given to pay the pledge. Note any dedication opportunities in the donation range they are considering.

Once individuals make a pledge, confirm it by letter. Be sure the letter is signed by either the individual making the phone call or the chair of the campaign committee.

Special Events

Church members like to participate in celebratory opportunities. Begin each capital campaign with a campaign kickoff event. This event should not be held until the potential large givers have made their pledges, which should total at least half of the funds needed. Plan this event carefully:

- Do not charge for this event.
- Find a company or a family that will pick up the cost of the food.
- The events subcommittee can recommend the time of day, the program, and the type of food served (for example, dinner or hors d'oeuvres).

The capital campaign kickoff is important to set the tone for the entire campaign. The event can follow this structure:

- Begin the event with a prayer from the minister.
- The council chair introduces the campaign committee chair and the building committee chair.
- The architect's rendering of the final building is shown.
- The church choir leads the congregation in favorite songs.
- A list of naming opportunities is distributed.
- The individuals who already made major pledges are introduced.
- It is helpful to have a speaker the congregants would like to hear, such as a political figure, sports figure, well-known minister, or television personality.
- Inform all attendees that they will be visited or called by a church volunteer to make their pledge and they are requested to make a generous pledge.

Time Limit to Pay Pledge

Decide on the time limit. Some campaigns have a three-year limit; some have five. Remember the tradeoff: the longer the pledge period, the more will be raised. However, the longer the pledge period, the more interest the church must pay a bank to borrow the necessary funds to pay bills as they become due.

Be sure to keep the church council and the church membership aware of all steps taken in the capital campaign. The more excitement that can be can generated, the larger the pledges will be.

Faith-Based Grant Writing

Many churches have been very successful in securing grants from the four major grant sources—government agencies, foundations, businesses, and individuals. It certainly is advantageous to be awarded a grant, because the church does not have to return the money. If the church takes out a loan, it must not only return the funds, but it must return them within a specific period of time and pay interest.

When looking for governmental funds, begin by checking eligibility. Some government agencies will not make grants to religious organizations at all. Others will give funds only to churches that have received 501(c)(3) nonprofit status from the Internal Revenue Service.

Government agencies have other restrictions on the use of funds. One common restriction is that if a church accepts grant funds, it must include individuals of all religions (or no religion) and not discriminate in any way in the provision of services. Once a church is eligible for governmental funding, there are few restrictions on the use of the funds. The only common restriction is that no funds can be used for religious services of any kind. Though this provision is clear, there is a dispute whether requiring individuals to attend religious services even though no governmental funds are used to provide them is legal. One idea that has been suggested is to offer religious services, but permit a waiver to any program participant who does not wish to attend.

These are controversial issues. Churches are advised to consult with their attorneys before applying for governmental grants.

Another area in which a church should check with its attorney relates to hiring restrictions. It is clear that a church cannot discriminate in hiring employees based on race. It is not clear, however, whether the church is permitted to hire only individuals in their own faith. May the church refuse to interview athiests or homosexuals? These issues have not been determined by the courts.

Funds received from other sources have fewer restrictions. Businesses, foundations, and individuals can give funds to a church, and the church may restrict participation in the programs to church members. However, it is not at all clear which other restrictions would apply.

One other major provision is in the use of the funds. A church wishing to raise funds to reduce the church's deficit would have to make certain the funding source would permit the funds to be used for this purpose.

Begin by obtaining the instructions from the funding source, referred to as the Request for Proposal (RFP). Follow these instructions carefully. Most RFPs request the following information.

Need

All funding sources have limited funds, so it is important to convince the potential funder of the need for the particular services your church would be providing. Try to quantify the need. In certain situations, it might be advisable to conduct a survey to determine the need. How many families would send their children to a daycare center at the church if one were offered? How about an after-school program? A waiting list for a particular service would be an indication of need.

Objectives

What would be the specific objectives or accomplishments if the program is funded? Again, make certain the objectives are quantifiable. How many individuals are expected to be served in the shelter each night? How many meals will be served? How many children will attend the daycare center?

Be sure the objectives are time-based. How many individuals are expected to be served in a month, a quarter, or a year? Be realistic. Do not make up numbers. Remember that if the proposal gets funded, you will be required to meet your objectives.

Activities

State the activities of the program in detail. For example, if the proposal is to operate a daycare center, include a daily schedule. Be sure to list the hours the program would be in operation.

Evaluation

How will you know if the objectives have been met? One way is to take a survey of program participants. Be sure to indicate that attendance will be taken at each program operated with grant funds.

Budget

Provide the funding source with a detailed and realistic budget:

- Salaries.
- Fringe benefits.
- Consumable supplies.
- Rent.
- Equipment.
- Telephone.

Letters of Support

Include in the application different kinds of letters supporting the program from:

- Potential users of the service.
- Other social service agencies with whom you will work.
- Religious organizations in the community with whom you will cooperate.

Ask the individuals writing the letters to make them as specific as possible. Exactly how will the community be helped if the grant is funded?

Special Tips for Church Grants

Keep the books for grants totally separate from the church books. Keep the funds in separate bank accounts with separate checkbooks. If church employees will be paid from grant funds, keep separate work records. If any individual is being paid part-time from grant funds, be sure to document the time spent working on grant-funded projects.

Be sure every employee and every program participant knows the policies to be followed regarding the separation of church and state. For example, if governmental funds are used, make certain that no proselytizing is permitted. Do not risk losing the grant; interpret these restrictions strictly.

Establish a separate board of directors for the grant. The church board and the grant board should function independently, even though some individuals may serve on both boards. Try to make the grant board as diverse as possible. Include individuals from different religions, ages, and backgrounds. It is recommended the grant board include clients, past clients, and families of clients.

Applying for Corporate Funds

Joy Skjegstad gives an excellent checklist of "Characteristics of Corporate Funders."[1] This list is equally important when considering foundation funding. These characteristics include:

- Strong ties to geography. Both corporations and foundations are much more likely to give funds to your church when they are located in your community.

- Employer involvement. This is such an important feature of successful grants that many churches begin their fundraising with it. They ask the employers of the members of the church council and the fundraising committee for grant funds.

- Concerns about giving to faith-based efforts. Skjegstad says "giving to faith-based groups may anger or alienate stakeholders who subscribe to a different religion or who practice no religion at all."[2] She therefore recommends asking corporate donors to fund only church programs that "had no faith content at all."[3]

  Another option is to ask potential corporate or foundation donors if they will consider making a grant to the church for religious purposes. Sometimes, a small business owner is a member of your church or denomination and will be pleased to make a grant to the church.

Many foundations state on their Website that they are willing to give grants to specific religious denominations. The most important step is to determine the policies of the donor before applying for funds.

- Ties to the core goals of the corporation. This is important. Learn the priorities of the foundation or business. Then submit an application consistent with them. For example, if a foundation funds children's programs, submit an application to that foundation for a church program to feed hungry children. If a business has a history of funding arts programs, ask it to fund your church's arts program.

  Be sure to apply to corporations that benefit from connections to your church. For example, apply for grants from undertakers and monument companies as well as companies that sell prayer books and other goods and services your church might buy. Any of your church's major suppliers should be considered for grant possibilities.

Look for Foundation Funds

One series of legal rulings that can help churches states that private individuals have broad leeway in giving away their wealth. Many of the restrictions that apply to government agencies funding churches do not apply to grants from foundations and individuals.

Look for foundations that have given money to churches of your denomination. Your local library is a good place to start in your search for foundation funds. Many libraries subscribe to on-line publications providing grant sources.

Grants From Judicatories

Many regional judicatories and national denominational offices make grants to the churches they serve. They may also make loans for construction and other causes. Some denominations are related to fraternal insurance companies, and these insurance companies may make loans and grants.

Churches Applying for Grants

One important consideration to make when your church is providing social services and seeking grants is whether to form a separate nonprofit organization. Joy Skjegstad, in *Starting a Nonprofit at Your Church,* recommends several reasons to form a separate organization if you are seeking grants. They include:

- Increasing the chances of raising funds from agencies and individuals who would not give grants to your church.

- Increasing the opportunity to recruit volunteers who would not volunteer for your church.

- Increasing the opportunity to recruit board members with needed expertise.

- Increasing the opportunity to collaborate with other organizations.

- Increasing the ability to make decisions more rapidly.

- Insulating the nonprofit from the politics and personalities of the church.

- Insulating the church from legal and financial liability.[4]

Make certain to ask any potential funder whether the grant board must be separate from the church board and whether the church must obtain non-profit status under Section 501(c)(3) from the Internal Revenue Service.

In her excellent book *Winning Grants to Strengthen Your Ministry,* Skjegstad gives a "readiness checklist" to see if your church is prepared to write grants. As her number-one item, she lists "you have incorporated as a 501(c)(3) organization." Her reasoning is very practical: "Foundations and corporations are less and less likely to consider a grant proposal if the organization hasn't incorporated as a 501(c)(3) nonprofit organization."[5]

Another reason for churches to set up a separate organization and apply to the IRS for nonprofit status under Section 501(c)(3) is to help ensure that the church does not cross the boundary between what a church can do and what a government-funded organization can do. Religious objectives and secular ones must be kept separate when governmental funds are involved.

National Faith-Based Funding Initiative

One important expansion of the ability of churches to obtain grant funds for their social service programs was the formation by President George W. Bush in 2001 of the Faith-Based Funding Initiative. President Barack Obama continued the program in 2009.[6]

A recent publication of the Center for Faith-Based and Neighborhood Partnerships cleared up some of the questions about funding for churches. One important statement was that no extra funds were being allocated for faith-based groups. The major change was that churches "are eligible to apply for governmental grants on an equal basis with other similar groups."[7]

Another important statement is there is no federal requirement that a church either incorporate or obtain nonprofit status under 501(c)(3) of the Internal Revenue Code.[8] However, many specific government agencies and foundations may require incorporation or nonprofit status. The faith-based initiatives publication emphasized that "Grant funds may not be used for inherently religious activities such as worship, prayer, proselytizing, or devotional Bible study."[9] One question the faith-based funding office did not address was whether religious groups can receive governmental money and restrict hiring to those in their particular religious faith. This is an issue that eventually will be decided by the courts.

13

Strategic Planning

Every church should have a plan for the future. Although almost everyone would agree in theory that having a plan is valuable, the vast majority of churches have never actually created a plan. There is no "right" way to plan. Every church is different. To quote a friend, "There are more than a million nonprofit organizations in America. And if you have seen one...you've seen one."

In 1965, Alvin J. Lindgren, in *Foundations for Purposeful Church Administration* made a powerful argument to "Strengthen the Church by Coordinated, Comprehensive Planning."[1] As Lindgren stated:

> It is easily observed that most churches do not engage in such systematic long-range planning. Perhaps this is one reason why the church has not been able to reach and change society more effectively. Many local churches operate on hand-to-mouth planning. They consider the pressing problems of the moment at each board meeting without placing them in proper perspective in relationship to either past or future.[2]

Nearly 50 years later, nothing has changed. The computer has been invented, congregants have e-mail, social networking has exploded, and still most congregations do not engage in coordinated, comprehensive planning.

The Planning Process

Begin the process by forming a planning committee as a standing committee of the church. The council chair appoints the chair of the planning committee. This individual should be a council member with the following characteristics:

- The respect of the congregation.
- The trust of the clergy.
- Some understanding of the group process.
- A grasp of the theoretical material.
- Leadership skills.
- Some experience in strategic planning in the business world.[3]

The planning committee chair appoints the members of the committee to represent a broad spectrum of church members, taking into consideration their:

- Gender.
- Age.
- Income.
- Length of time in community.

If possible, include some members who attend services "religiously" and others who attend rarely. Try to include members with different beliefs about the role of the church. The planning committee should be large enough to ensure a variety of views, but not too large as to be unwieldy. Perhaps a committee of 10 to 15 members would work. One essential requirement is that each member of the planning committee must commit to attending all meetings of the committee.

Sections of the Plan

At an early meeting, the committee should identify the major sections of the plan. They might include the following:

- Building.
- Worship.
- Assisting the minister.
- Fundraising.
- Programming.
- Church council.
- Helping those in need.

There is no set list. Select the topics of major interest to your church. The committee should be flexible; final sections of the plan will change as it is developed.

Getting Congregational Input

It is extremely important to get input from the parishioners. There are as many ways to do this as there are different churches.

Planning Session

One effective way is to call a "Church Planning Forum." Publicize the forum often and far in advance so you can have as large an attendance as possible.

Begin by having the chair of the planning committee explain the purpose of the meeting. Give out a list of the "breakout tables" that correspond to the sections of the plan. Then have all attendees move to the breakout table of their choice.

Each breakout table should have a preassigned table leader and note taker. Each table should have a flip chart. The table leader should say: "For the next hour, we will make recommendations to give to the planning committee for issues relating to the sections of the plan we have selected." As suggestions are made, the note taker lists them on the flip chart. At the end of the hour, all the groups reconvene. Table leaders then report on the recommendations of their groups, using the flip charts as a guide.

Church Input Meetings

Another option is to have a series of planning meetings at the church about different parts of the plan. One evening, a meeting is held for all those wanting to comment on the worship functions of the church; another evening, a meeting is held for those who want to discuss the short-term and long-term needs of the church building. Another meeting would be held to discuss church fundraising opportunities, and another would be held to focus on church programming.

Techniques for Gathering Information

Many churches survey all of their members. There are many ways to do this. Some send a questionnaire in the mail. Others find an e-mail survey is more effective. Still other congregations call church members on the phone. If a phone survey is used, many churches precede this with a note to congregants describing the survey and informing the congregants that they will get a call from a church volunteer.

Another technique is to hold focus groups. Identify a diverse group of 10 to 15 parishioners. Meet with them and ask questions about different sections of the strategic plan. Another method is to conduct in-person one-on-one interviews with a number of church members.

Obtaining information about present church programs can be combined with asking for information about church programs individuals would like to see in the future. Make sure to thank everyone participating in the planning process.

Beginning to Write the Plan

The planning committee should determine the length of the strategic plan. Should it be a three-year, five-year, or 10-year plan? Who will actually draft the plan? Will it be drafted by the minister, another staff member, or a member of the planning committee? How often and when should the planning committee meet? Whether the committee meets weekly or monthly, and whether it should meet in the evening or another part of the day is up to the committee.

Information Gathering

Begin by gathering information. It is interesting that the list outlined by Lindgren in 1965 is just as relevant today as it was then:

Studies of a local church should include an analysis of the following areas:

- Membership (growth, age-sex pyramid, infant baptisms, geographic location, length of membership).
- Leadership studies (age-sex distribution, number of positions, tenure of each office, distance from church, length of local church membership).
- Sunday worship attendance (charted weekly from an accurate count by ushers).

- Church school (membership, average attendance—total and by departments).

- Missions (regular missionary giving, special projects, women's society, and other groups, number of study or educational sessions each year).

- Finances (history of giving—total, local, building, benevolences, per capita analysis, age-sex giving distribution, history of community income change, number and amount of pledges annually).

- Community studies (population changes, school enrollment, neighborhood and housing changes, per capita income, community services).[4]

One essential part of planning today's and tomorrow's church is keeping detailed current demographics of its members electronically in its computer files. This information is useful not only for planning purposes, but also for many other aspects of church management.

Every church should have the e-mail addresses of its members. If church services are cancelled because of a major weather event, e-mails can then be sent to notify most of the members. Many notices and announcements can be sent by e-mail, thus saving significant sums in postage. Members can be informed of births, deaths, and other life-cycle events through e-mail.

If the church decides to note special occasions such as birthdays or anniversaries, this task is greatly simplified when demographics are kept on the computer. If the church wants to sponsor youth group programs for its members, a computer program can be used to compile a list of each child in delineated age ranges. Senior citizens can be invited to programs established for them.

Should the church sponsor a program for singles? How many singles between the ages of 16 and 40 belong to the church? How many singles are older than 40? How many church members are single parents? One important purpose of reviewing the demographics of church membership is to assist in future planning. If the congregation consists almost exclusively of senior citizens, the planning committee will make different recommendations than if the majority of members are younger than 40.

The planning committee should also review attendance at church services. Counting how many individuals attend regular weekly or holiday services is important in planning. It also is important to count how many individuals attend church educational programs and other church programs.

Making the Plan "Strategic"

A strategic plan takes into consideration not only the demographics of church membership, but also information about the community in which the church is located. Begin with information about existing and expected population growth. Often the county or local municipality in which the church is located is a good place to start. Obtain any planning reports that have been approved by municipal bodies. Obtain information about the age ranges of individuals living in your community. How does the percentage of elderly individuals compare with the percentage in your church? Is the elderly population expected to increase or decrease in the future? Determine the religious demographics of your community. How many churches of your denomination exist?

Writing the Plan

Begin the plan by describing the history of your church. When was it formed? Why was it formed? A section should be devoted to the mission and vision of the church. Often, the church judicatory body can give input into this process.

As the planning committee begins to draft the plan, make certain it is as specific as possible. Always start with a benchmark. If the committee recommends steps to increase attendance at Sunday worship services, begin by stating how many individuals attend now. If the goal is to increase receipts or decrease expenditures, what are the present budgetary figures? Make every objective measurable. Examples might be:

- Increase church membership from _____ to _____ by the year 20__.
- Begin a capital campaign to build an extension to the church in the year 20__.
- Increase the amount in the weekly collection offering from _____ to _____ by the year 20__.
- Begin a program for singles by the year 20__.

State who has the responsibility for implementing each recommendation. Some recommendations will be referred to the church building committee or the church membership committee. Others will be referred to the church council or the minister.

Possible Sections of the Plan

When writing a plan, it is important to include sections on building plans, fundraising, and social ministry.

Building Plans

Building plans should begin with a detailed tour of the church. Which repairs should be done this year? Which repairs should be done next year? What year should the roof be replaced? (Replacements and repairs should be made before they are desperately needed. Waiting for the roof to leak on a congregant in a future rainstorm is unacceptable.) Does the church need a complete refurbishing? Does the church need a new addition?

Remember that the committee is planning not only for the existing church but for the church of the future. If the plan envisions a 50-percent increase in attendance at the church school in the next five years, plan now for that increase.

The sanctuary must always be large enough to seat everyone who wants to pray. However, building an extension when church attendance is expected to decrease is not good planning.

Fundraising

All churches can use more funds. There are many techniques that can be used to acquire them. Give a list of options and get input from the congregants about each. See Chapter 9 of this book for a discussion of options. Consider each one. Here are a few:

- Fundraising dinner.
- Memorial program.
- Donations to the church.
- Special events.

Social Ministry

Every church has as part of its mission helping those in need. This includes helping individuals who are members of the church, the needy in the community, and those who need help around the world. Many churches participate in "crop walks" or programs sponsored by the church's denominational office.

Some churches have a direct connection with social service agencies sponsored by their faith body. For example, Catholic churches often work directly with Catholic Social Services in their communities. Others work directly with social service agencies in the community, such as Habitat for Humanity or the local food bank. In some communities, churches join together to help the needy by jointly sponsoring a food kitchen or a shelter, for example.

An essential part of planning is to develop and publicize a method for church members in need to get help. Decide what steps individuals should take who are in need of food, shelter, or counseling. For example, should they notify the minister or the chair of the social ministries committee?

Approving the Plan

Once the strategic plan has been drafted, it should be reviewed by the church council. It is recommended that a separate meeting of the council be held to discuss the plan, rather than just adding such a discussion to the busy agenda of a regular meeting.

Send the draft plan to all council members well before the meeting and ask them to read it carefully. Perhaps members of the planning committee can present different chapters of the plan at a council meeting. The planning committee should then meet to discuss the council's recommendations. The plan should be redrafted and sent to the council for final approval.

Plan Follow-Up

Once the plan has been approved by the council, the planning committee should continue to meet. It should begin by thinking through how the plan's recommendations can be implemented. If the plan includes new ways of budgeting, the planning committee might meet with the church's finance committee to implement those recommendations. Changes in ritual should be discussed with the worship committee and the minister.

It is important for the planning committee to review the plan at least once a quarter to see how it is being implemented. At the end of each year, the planning committee should redraft the plan so that it is always current.

Membership and Programming

Two important functions of churches are increasing membership and keeping existing members happy.

New Members

The church bulletin and periodic letters from the council chair should remind all church members that everyone should be looking for potential new members.

It is important to have a membership committee. All church members are encouraged to fill out a form and send it to the membership committee chair when they see a potential church-going family. They should include the following information:

- Name and approximate ages of all the adults in the household.
- Name and approximate ages of all the children in the household.
- Relationship to the family being recommended (neighbor, work-related).
- Time lived in community.
- Religious affiliation, if any.
- Address of potential member.
- Phone number of potential member.
- E-mail address of potential member.
- Name of individual filling out form.
- Telephone number of individual filling out form.
- Date.

The next step would be for a member of the membership committee to call the potential new members by phone. Find out their interests, so you can:

- Mail them a church brochure giving them general information about church activities.
- Put them on the mailing list to receive the church bulletin.
- Put them on the church weekly e-mail list to get current information about church programs.
- Add them to the church mailing list to receive hard-copy information about church programs.
- Invite them to join you at a church service.
- Ask if they would like you to set up a meeting with the minister to take a tour of the church and learn about the range of church activities.
- Depending on the ages of the family members, invite individuals to different church events. A young person would be invited to a youth group meeting; a senior citizen would be invited to a senior citizens' discussion group.
- Inquire if they would be interested in learning about the church's various volunteer activities.

Rick Warren, in his best-selling book *The Purpose Driven Church*, includes several tips for the membership committee. His list of greeting potential new members at church services is an excellent one. He recommends your church:

- Reserve the best parking spots for visitors.
- Station greeters outside your building.
- Set up information tables outside your building.
- Place directional signs everywhere.
- Have taped music playing when people enter your building.
- Allow visitors to remain anonymous during the service.
- If you use a registration card, have everyone fill one out.

- Offer a public welcome that relaxes people.
- Begin and end each service with people greeting each other.
- If you use name tags, make sure everybody gets one.
- Offer a refreshment table at each service.[1]

The membership committee often develops an individualized plan for each potential new member. Demographics are important. An adult with young children might contact another family with young children and invite them to sit with them at services next Sunday. An individual who lives on the same street might make the initial call. If the church has a youth group, a young person of the same age might make the call. In some instances, the minister might make the initial contact, or the educational director could invite parents to bring their child to a Sunday School class.

In many situations, it may be better to strike up a friendship with the new family without mentioning the church. Maybe after inviting the new family over for dinner, they may ask for recommendations of a church to join. Asking the new family to join you for church services may not be the right approach. The family might first get involved through a youth sports team or attending an adult education program.

It is also important to give businesses that cater to newcomers the brochure from your church. Real estate agents, for example, are often asked for information about the churches in a particular community. Prospective new members should be added to the list of congregants receiving regular e-mails about church programs. The church's Website should be updated frequently and should be mentioned frequently in communications. The minister's sermon should be posted on the Website. The church should keep current with the newest social networking techniques.

Appoint a welcome subcommittee of the membership committee. Any "stranger" who attends church services should be greeted by a member of the welcome subcommittee. Obtain information about the individual attending services for the first time, including name, address, phone number, e-mail address, and names and ages of other members of the family. See Appendix 6 for a form visitors can fill out when they attend church services.

Procedures should be developed for greeting individuals who stop in at the church during business hours. Of course, it is important to give potential members a brochure about the church, and every church should have one. A one page brochure, "Welcome to Holy Spirit Catholic Church," contains the following information about the church:

- Address.
- Phone number.
- Website.
- Picture of church.
- Welcome statement.
- Listing of "service-oriented ministries."
- History.
- Information about new church under construction.
- Background of pastor.
- Picture of pastor.
- Information about Catholic faith.
- Time of masses.
- Time of confession.[2]

All church staff members should know basic facts about the church to discuss with anyone who asks questions. How many children are enrolled in the Sunday School? When was the church founded? How much does it cost to rent the church hall for a wedding?

Most individuals who stop in at a church would like to meet the minister. If the minister is not there, be sure the minister is given information about the visitor in order to follow up. Be sure to make the family welcome. The membership committee should have the responsibility of coordinating contacts with all potential members.

Joining the Church

One important function of a church is to decide who is a "member." To be a member of a local Methodist Church means joining a worldwide fellowship of Methodists. "These vows are considered to be a kind of covenant with God and with the members of the local church, and they are made in response to five basic questions, which are asked of all persons seeking membership, in the presence of the congregation."[3] In many synagogues, the rabbi determines who is "Jewish" and who thus qualifies for synagogue membership. Different branches of Judaism have different rules for determining who is Jewish. In some churches, all a member must do to join is to fill out a form. If the church has a system of dues, it is important to have in place a system for waiving or reducing the dues payment for families who cannot afford to pay the full amount.

Thom Rainer, in his book *High Expectations: The Remarkable Secret for Keeping People in Your Church,* stresses the importance of "new member classes" or "prospective member classes" in excellent churches. The church council must decide whether attendance in these classes is mandatory or voluntary for new members. Rainer also stresses that the "high expectation churches" review the content of these classes on a regular basis to be sure the content is current and interesting. Rainer's study indicated that "churches that require membership class attendance prior to membership have significantly higher retention rates than other churches."[4] Appendix 8 indicates topics included in Rainer's study of "high expectation churches."

Rick Warren suggests three separate classes for new members of different ages:

- Older elementary kids.
- Junior high and high school.
- Adults.[5]

Having a plan to attract new members is important. Though you do not want to stop individuals from praying at your church because they are not members, you should point out the advantages of church membership to every visitor. When new members join the church, it is important to inform them of the responsibilities of membership. Appendix 7 provides an excellent example of a church membership form.

Be sure to have a plan for special welcomes for all new members. Honoring them at a dinner, welcoming them in the church bulletin, or introducing them at church services can all be effective.

Existing Members

A "member services" subcommittee of the membership committee should be charged with the task of ensuring all members get maximum services:

- Members who are in the hospital are visited.
- Members who are homebound are visited.
- Members who have lost a loved one are visited in their bereavement.

If members have not attended church services for a while, they should receive a call from a representative of the member services subcommittee to encourage church attendance and to see if the church can provide any special services for them.

Consider a number of steps Rainer recommends for keeping people in your church. Successful churches have a policy for follow-up with every new church member. Church leaders make certain that new members are "touched" in a number of ways. The follow-up may involve a personal letter from the pastor, a telephone call, or perhaps a visit to the home of the person who came to church.[6]

Another effective tool for retaining members is what Rainer calls a "greeter ministry."[7] The membership committee can decide the specifics of the roles of the individuals who greet individuals attending church services, whether they wear name tags, and whether they should be located in the parking lot, at the front door, or at all entrance doors of the church.[8]

Expanding Church Programs

In this technological age, the church's computer should include detailed, up-to-date demographic information about every church member. The appropriate church members should be notified of every relevant church activity.

Remember that not every congregant has an e-mail address. Though notices can be sent by e-mail, the same notice must be sent by U.S. mail to those who do not have an e-mail address.

It is important to ask members of the congregation from time to time which church programs they would like to attend. This can be done by a mail survey, an e-mail survey, or by telephone. Another technique is to list several specific programs and ask church members if they are interested. For example, ask members if they would like to participate in a social action committee, an interfaith dialogue committee, or a worship committee. Some churches send congregants a list of all committees periodically and ask members to sign up for committees in which they have an interest.

Another function of the membership committee is contacting individuals who resign from church membership. These individuals should receive a phone call from a representative of the membership committee thanking them for their past membership. If they have been unhappy with the church, find out why. In many situations, an angry family may make untrue statements to others in the community. Proper handling of a dispute may minimize the chances of this occurring. It is extremely important to speak to a family who did not like the minister and ask why, rather than relying on rumor and hearsay. It is also important to keep accurate records of why families leave the church. If most families leave because they are moving out of the community, the membership committee will act differently than if the families did not like the minister's sermons.

Expanding Programming for Special Interest Groups

Two things are clear in the 21st-century church. First, "one size fits all" does not work. Too many churches spend all their time concentrating on offering worship services to all congregants, which is surely a worthy task. But different members of the church have different spiritual needs, and special efforts must be taken to meet these needs. Also, in our complex world, individual groups can be reached in specific ways that will not work for other groups. Reaching young people with social networks such as Facebook, Twitter, and text messages will work; however, many senior citizens do not even have e-mail addresses.

Second, what also does not work in the "new" church is the traditional method of giving a constituent group a "seat on council" and then assuming that individual will speak for the group. Putting a young person on the council, even if that particular individual attends all the meetings, will not automatically lead to serving all the young people in the congregation.

What *does* work in the 21st-century church? The membership committee should keep accurate records of the demographics of church members. If a church has a large number of single mothers with young children, for example, the church should offer specific programming for this demographic. Knowing how many single young people belong to the church is very important when developing programming.

Try identifying all the individuals in a particular group, inviting them to a meeting, and asking them how the church can meet their needs. Larry Osborne suggests giving the groups special names. He calls the young people "Young Eagles."[9] Start by identifying a few "Young Eagles" and having them meet with the staff or council person who will be the liaison to the group from the church leadership.

Note that your church computer records should sort the e-mail addresses of everyone in the church by different age groupings. The planning committee should recommend the age group to be invited. Pick a place and time for the initial meeting. Again, different groups have different needs. Some groups are comfortable meeting in the church; others hold the meeting in a private home. Some groups meet in the evening; others meet at breakfast, lunch, or right after work.

For the initial meeting, send an e-mail message to those with e-mail addresses and a hard-copy invitation to those who have no e-mail. State that the purpose of the meeting is to call together individuals with common interests to see how the church can better serve their needs. Encourage those receiving the notice to invite others in their group whether they are church members or not. For the first meeting, a member of their age group should make personal phone calls to encourage attendance.

The original planning group should hold several meetings to identify different "constituents." In addition to young people in general, other groups might be

- Young singles.
- Parents of young children.
- Parents of teenagers.
- Single parents.

- Empty nesters.
- Senior citizens.
- Intermarried couples.
- Parents with intermarried children.
- Individuals who have recently lost a spouse.

At the First Meeting

The meeting should be led by an individual who is a member of that constituency. The member of the church staff or board assigned to the group should also attend. Begin by passing around a sign-up sheet to obtain information about all the attendees. Then ask everyone to share information with the full group. How long have they lived in the community? Are they church members? What are their interests? Then guide the discussion to how the church can help them. Would they like to continue to meet as a "special group?" If so, set the date, time, place, and agenda for the next meeting. Remember to offer refreshments at all meetings.

Do not make the mistake of discussing only "religious" needs. If a group wants to get together to meet purely social needs, that is fine. If the "young singles" want to have a dance, help them organize a dance. Offer them the church hall at no charge and show them how to operate the church's sound equipment. Perhaps the group may be given several choices and again, the choices may be purely social. Perhaps the group may want to go to a baseball game or a concert together.

Of course, activities may be related to religious topics. How about a book club that reviews a book with religious themes or the discussion of a political topic with religious dimensions? A meeting to discuss a religious issue such as the importance of Vatican II to the Catholic Church or a meeting with a Holocaust survivor to discuss his faith would be in order.

The discussion leader should try to encourage participation from all attendees. Often one individual dominates the meeting and the others are hesitant to give their opinions. Do not vote on anything. Be sure to decide on an activity only if it is agreed to by everyone or nearly everyone in the room. Remember that the decisions must be made by the group. The staff member should be available to answer questions and take minutes, if asked to do so. These minutes should include only the decisions made by the group.

15

Getting and Keeping Volunteers

Every church relies on volunteer assistance. Many other non-profit agencies may exist without volunteers, but no effective churches do. Whereas the ratio of paid staff to volunteers in a typical nonprofit organization might be 2 to 1, many churches have more than 100 volunteers for each paid staff member. The potential for recruiting volunteers for the church is great. Volunteering for religious organizations is more common than for any other kind of organization.[1] It is essential, therefore, for each church to have a well-planned system for the effective use of volunteers.

An important place to begin is with a job description for every volunteer position in the church. This would include council members, committee members, special project volunteers, office volunteers, and volunteers who assist in religious services such as choir members. Every volunteer job description would include the following:

- Title of position (assistant secretary, member of choir, kitchen aide).
- Position qualifications.
- Examples of duties.
- Degrees or certificates required (if any).
- Hours required each week.
- Location of position (church, home).
- Name of supervisor.
- Special requirements (driver's license, car insurance).
- Any additional information about the position.

Application

Every member of the congregation should be given a list of the job descriptions. A sample volunteer job description is included as Appendix 11. A special church bulletin entitled "Opportunities to Help the Church" might be a good way to accomplish this. Another excellent suggestion is for church members to fill out a listing of their skills and interests. A Talent Bank Questionnaire is included as Appendix 12. Every individual who wants to volunteer should be asked to fill out an application with the following information:

- Name.
- Street address.
- City, state, zip.
- Daytime telephone number.
- Evening telephone number.
- E-mail address.
- Emergency contact name.
- Emergency contact phone number.
- Skills and interests.
- Position(s) applied for.
- Experience in similar positions in other organizations.

Every individual who applies for a volunteer position should be interviewed. If possible, the interview should be conducted by the individual who would be the volunteer's supervisor. This could be a paid staff member such as the minister, or a volunteer such as the chair of the ritual committee. The interviewer should give specific examples of the type of work each volunteer would be expected to perform. In some instances, volunteers will be told on the spot that the church would be pleased to have them serve in a specific position and what the next step would be. In other situations, potential volunteers will be told that the interviewer will get back to them. In the latter instance, make certain to get back to the volunteer shortly. Make every effort to accept volunteers in all areas where they want to help.

After the interview, the interviewer should write down his/her impression of each applicant. Did he/she have the requirements for the position? Does the interviewer have to get back to the volunteer?

Orientation

Every volunteer should be required to participate in two orientation programs. One is a general orientation for every church volunteer, which should be held several times during the year. This should include:

- Welcome by the council chair.
- Welcome by the minister.
- Information about the church.
- General rules of conduct.
- Emergency procedures and telephone numbers.
- Listing of important phone numbers (for example, minister's home phone number).
- Appropriate dress.
- Appropriate and inappropriate language.
- Rules relating to the use of alcoholic beverages.
- Rules relating to smoking.
- Rules of confidentiality.
- Use of church telephones and computers.
- Steps to take if the volunteer is unable to attend a scheduled activity, such as driving a parishioner to a doctor's appointment.
- Specific rules (for example, drivers must have a valid driver's license and insurance).
- Listing of the IRS mileage rate for volunteers.
- Procedures to follow if there are disputes.
- Rules for the use of the church kitchen.
- How to obtain church keys.
- How the church burglar alarm works.

At a different time, each volunteer receives information about specific tasks. This session is usually headed by their supervisor and includes:

- Written information on the specific tasks.
- Whom to contact if they cannot meet their commitment.

- Names, addresses, and phone numbers of fellow volunteers and supervisors.
- Written time commitments.
- Procedures for asking questions or offering suggestions.

Volunteer Information

Every volunteer should be evaluated using the same procedures as those for the paid staff as outlined in Chapter 3. It is important to develop a folder for each volunteer. It should include:

- Application form.
- Emergency contact information.
- Time records.
- Evaluations.

Keep active records of volunteer service. Include records of the number of hours each individual has volunteered. This is important when recognition awards are given out. In that way, a volunteer would be given special recognition for accomplishments such as heading a committee for 10 years or helping in the office for 500 hours. Record-keeping is also important when recruiting for additional volunteers. It will also be useful when applying for faith-based grants.

Keep in a file the special needs of individual volunteers. Note if there any problems. For example, assigning a particular volunteer to drive a parishioner to a doctor's appointment would not be appropriate if his/her record noted the volunteer rarely showed up for specific assignments.

Volunteer Recognition

It is important to take advantage of numerous opportunities to thank volunteers:

- Be sure to thank all members of a committee when giving a committee report.
- At any special event, make certain to distribute a written program listing the volunteers for that event.
- Highlight the contributions of volunteers in each church bulletin.

- Make certain to thank volunteers at an annual church appreciation event.

- At least once each year, and more often if appropriate, be sure to send all volunteers a note thanking them for their service.

- Thank volunteers for each five years of service in any volunteer capacity—council officer, council member, chair of committee, member of an active committee.

A comprehensive list of ways to thank volunteers is provided in Appendix 13. A church bulletin provides a wonderful opportunity to praise the work of volunteers and thank them. Highlight one volunteer in every issue. Include their picture so all congregants can recognize them. Give their background, the community where they grew up, and how long they have lived in your community. List all the volunteer tasks they perform for the church. Include a paragraph about their special skills. Tell about their family members. List their "day job." Quote the minister or another volunteer praising them for their skills.

Use the church bulletin to list specific tasks that need volunteers. If the church choir needs additional members, for example, outline that specific need. Inform the congregation of the skills needed. List the training provided. State when auditions will be held. State when the choir meets for practice and when the choir performs. If the congregation needs office assistance, list that in the church bulletin as well. For example, the church office may need help with major mailings. Put in the bulletin approximately how often such help is needed and for how many hours. If any specific skills are needed, such as computer skills, list those, too.

Another use of the church bulletin is to thank volunteers. Every time a specific task is performed, such as preparing a church dinner, thank the volunteers who helped prepare it. Be sure not to leave anyone's name off the list and that everyone's name is included as they would like to see it, and spell all names correctly. Some individuals are Kathy, some Cathy, some Cathleen, some Kathleen, and there are many other variations. You may hurt an individual's feelings if you list his name as Bill when he would prefer to be referred to as William, Will, Willy, Billy, or Skip.

It is recommended to have volunteer recognition events during the year. You can often combine these with a fundraiser for the church. Check with volunteers to see what would be appropriate. Some congregations have a lunch at the end of a particular church service. Others have breakfasts or dinners throughout the year to honor volunteers. Honoring young people for their volunteer service is especially important. They need to know that their service is appreciated by adults in general and their church in particular. Include volunteers in celebratory events such as holiday parties. Be sure to have social events during the year to which volunteers are invited.

At each recognition event, make certain to pronounce every volunteer's name correctly. If there is a question, ask individuals how their names are pronounced. Also ask how they wish to be recognized in mailings. Some women prefer to be recognized as Ms. Jane Smith, some as Mrs. Jane Smith, and others as Mrs. John Smith. Some individuals prefer to include letters indicating advanced educational degrees, such as MSW or MD. Some include letters indicating professional achievements such as A.F.R.E. For example, the author of this book is Michael Alan Sand. He would not be upset if either Michael Sand or Mike Sand is thanked for volunteer service. He does not care if his middle name or initial is included. However, he does get upset when Michael Sand<u>s</u> is thanked. We would not even recognize a reference to Rev. Martin Luther King, Jr. as Marty King or even Martin King. We might know who William Jefferson Clinton is, but Bill Clinton is rarely referred to that way.

Be sure every volunteer has a mentor. This is an individual with extensive volunteering experience. Newer volunteers will know they can turn to this individual with questions or complaints. Mentors should be called on to thank the individual they have mentored.

Dealing With Difficult Volunteers

One problem with an organization like a church that relies on a large number of volunteers is that not every volunteer is excellent. With any large number of volunteers, it can be expected that a small percentage will engage in conduct that is not acceptable.

Unfortunately, too many individuals believe that because a volunteer does not get paid, poor behavior must be tolerated by the organization. This is not true. The first step in the process is to inform paid staff and all volunteers that every volunteer represents the church and certain conduct is unacceptable. The volunteer orientation is a good place to make this statement.

Clarify which specific behaviors are not acceptable. For example, many tasks require the individual be at the church at a particular time. Be sure the volunteer is certain when specific time attendance is expected. In some cases, a follow up e-mail confirming the date and time may be sent. Be sure volunteers know whom to contact, and by when, if they cannot attend a meeting or perform a particular task.

One way to deal with lack of attendance is to follow up each time a volunteer misses an important assignment. For example, if a volunteer was supposed to drive a congregant to the doctor and simply did not show up, an e-mail or call from the supervisor would be in order. Remind volunteers again what steps should be taken if they cannot fulfill an assignment.

Document unacceptable behavior. Be specific. If individuals do not perform specific services they promised to perform, document this. If they use inappropriate language, write down the specific words used. Then have the volunteer's supervisor meet with the volunteer in a quiet place. Do not use general negative language. Just point to specific examples of the inappropriate behavior. If possible, give specific examples of what appropriate behavior would be.

Be specific, but do not denigrate the volunteer. If a volunteer has had many accidents, for example, it is appropriate to say that he/she cannot drive children on Sunday School trips. Go out of your way, however, to provide other opportunities for the volunteer to interact with the children. If a volunteer's voice is such that he/she can no longer sing in the church choir, thank the volunteer for prior service. In most instances, the volunteer will realize that his/her church choir days have ended and will not be upset.

Think carefully about whether to involve the minister. In some instances, the minister would be the most effective individual to encourage a particular volunteer to improve his/her conduct. In other instances, especially if no religious issues are involved, including the minister in this type of discussion with a volunteer would not be appropriate.

Volunteers who say they will change their conduct should be given an opportunity to do. This may be the best solution to the problem. However, if inappropriate behavior continues, it may be necessary to inform volunteers that they can no longer be given a particular assignment.

Committee on Volunteers

One important idea is to form a committee on volunteers. Marlene Wilson, in her book *How to Mobilize Church Volunteers*, recommends that the members of this committee should not only be knowledgeable about the church and its members, but also should be committed to a fuller utilization of the gifts of all members. The individual should agree to consider the committee a priority and attend meetings at least once a month.[2]

This committee would perform all the tasks outlined in this chapter:

- Prepare a list of volunteer tasks.
- Interview and assign volunteers.
- Look for specific volunteers for particular tasks.
- Keep volunteer records.
- Coordinate volunteer orientation and recognition events.

Make the statement in the church bulletin or at church services that the committee on volunteers would like to offer every member of the congregation the opportunity to volunteer to help the church. The next step would be to publicize the list of volunteer tasks and the list of committees and committee assignments. Then contact each member of the congregation by e-mail, by phone, or in person, and ask them to tell you about their interests and skills. See if you can match them up with a particular volunteer opportunity. By using this procedure, every congregant will feel that his/her skills, whatever they are, can be used by the congregation. In addition, the number of volunteers undertaking tasks or serving on committees will be greatly increased.

The committee on volunteers can also publicize opportunities for assisting individuals in the church who need help in the general community or in the world. If a parishioner needs assistance with meals or shopping, that individual would be informed how to get the help.

Set up a system for notifying the church if an individual is in the hospital or would like a home visit. Be sure the minister and a member of the appropriate committee visit the parishioner.

Youth groups must have adult supervision. Think through what type of adult assistance is needed. Teenagers, for example, may be able to decide on their own projects and carry them out with minimal supervision. They must be reminded, however, that they are representatives of the church.

Helping the community is part of the mission of many churches. Some are connected with faith-based organizations such as Catholic Charities, Lutheran Social Services, or the Methodist Home for the Aged. A church may work with a particular nonprofit in the community. This may be a food bank, a homeless shelter, or a youth group. These nonprofits may have volunteering needs that occur on a regular basis. The needs may also be calendar-based, such as an annual children's Christmas party.

Surveys have shown that involvement in the church encourages people to think about volunteering to help the needy. At least 75 percent of those who attend religious services participate in congregations that sponsor social service activities of one kind or other, meaning that most congregants have an opportunity to volunteer.[3]

Matching individuals who wish to provide help with those who wish to receive it is an important part of each church's mission.

Meaningful Life-Cycle Events

One important reason for joining a church is to participate in life-cycle events. Whether the event is a birth, a confirmation ceremony, a wedding, or a death, individuals find that participating in a church ritual to note the event is important.

Funerals

Most churches do not have written procedures for marking life-cycle events at the church. When an individual experiences the death of a loved one, the event is often made even more stressful if there are no clear written instructions about how to proceed. It is unfortunate when the congregant finds the church closed and minister's home phone number unlisted. Thus, it is essential for every church to have a booklet with complete information regarding the procedures to be followed on the death of a congregant or a congregant's loved one. Who should be called when? What steps should you take if you have already purchased a cemetery plot? What if you have not?

The relationship between a church and the funeral home should be spelled out clearly in writing. What are the duties of the church minister? What services are provided by the funeral home? Does the congregant have a choice of funeral homes?

Who makes choices about caskets and hearses, and what are the options? Who sends the obituary to the local paper? To the editor of the church bulletin? What information should be included?

What about the cemetery? Does the congregant contact the cemetery? Does the funeral home? The chair of the cemetery committee? Does the minister? How are procedures different if the deceased has requested cremation? Again, spell out these policies in detail in advance and in writing. Booklets about the funeral practices of a particular religion are helpful to congregants. For a Catholic experiencing a death, reading *Preparing a Catholic Funeral* is important.[1]

Births

Procedures for church rituals relating to a birth should be written in simple language and distributed to all church members. A mother with a newborn in a hospital should have to worry about as few things as possible. What are the religious options? Different churches will have different rules for baptism. A synagogue should have written specific rules for the circumcision of a boy and the religious ceremony that accompanies it. The synagogue should provide written procedures for religious ceremonies when a girl is born.

Weddings

Procedures for the happy couple to follow should be spelled out in writing to assist both the minister and the family in their planning. Is it a requirement for the couple to meet with the minister when the engagement is announced? What are the church rules for intermarriage? Will the minister perform the wedding ceremony if the bride and groom are of different faiths?

What are the church's procedures for the wedding vows? What input does the couple have? Are wedding rings required or optional? Is there a dress code for the bride and groom?

It would be very helpful to list florists, caterers, bands, photographers, and other vendors recommended by the church.

Life-Cycle Procedures

At a minimum, each church should have a detailed form for a congregant to fill out when planning a life-cycle event. A form for weddings and funerals is included as Appendix 14.

Another important reason for spelling out the procedures in writing in advance is to give congregants an opportunity for input. If a congregant has a suggestion to make about a church procedure, waiting until a birth or death has occurred is not the ideal time to begin a discussion.

Congregants should be given an idea of costs of life-cycle events. A funeral can be extremely costly, and knowing the average costs well in advance can reduce the stress considerably. The family of a bride and groom also needs to plan for the wedding expenses, and knowing the cost of renting the church hall and the numerous other expenses is very helpful.

It is also important to note whether the services of the minister or the church's custodial staff are included as a benefit of church membership or have additional costs. If security is needed for an event at the church, outline its cost. Note the options available for items such as parking or cloak room attendants.

Written procedures for all life-cycle events should be outlined in as much detail as possible:

- Must the church's religious leader lead the wedding service? Can the couple select its own clergy?
- What are the alternatives for holding a wedding dinner at the church?
- What is the seating capacity of the church for religious services?
- What is the seating capacity of the church hall for meals?
- Are alcoholic beverages permitted?
- Are there any religious restrictions on the type of food that can be served?
- What are the catering options? Can the congregant select any outside caterer? Does the church provide an inside catering option?
- If some meals can be provided by a church catering committee, what are the costs of different menus?
- Can the church hall be rented out for wedding dinners for non-church members? Are the costs and the rules different from those for church members?

One important recommendation is that these procedures should be included on the church's Website as well as in a separate brochure. That way, congregants can access the procedures from their home computers.

The procedures should be reviewed at least annually by the special events committee of the church to ensure they are up-to-date. The more current the information provided to congregants, the better.

The Excellent Church, Synagogue, Mosque, or Temple

Whether you are a parishioner, the minister, the education director, or the music director, you want your religious institution to be excellent. Please go through this checklist and mark each question "yes" or "no." If you have marked "yes" to all 57 items, you have an excellent church! If most answers are marked "no," you have room for improvement. Think about what steps you can take to make the "no" items "yes."

Do not get discouraged. Change is difficult. Just do the best you can. I hope that reading this book will give you advice on steps to take to make your church excellent.

Hiring the Religious Leader

Does your church have:

1. Written procedures for hiring the religious leader?
2. Written procedures for forming a search committee to implement the procedures for hiring the religious leader?
3. A system of obtaining references as part of the search process?
4. A detailed church profile to give to each potential minister?

Supporting the Religious Leader

Does your church have:

5. Regularly scheduled meetings with the minister and senior staff?

6. Regularly scheduled meetings with the minister and the church council chair?

7. A group of parishioners with whom the minister meets to discuss ways of improving the church?

Evaluating the Religious Leader and Staff

Does your church have:

8. Job descriptions for the minister and all staff members that are reviewed on a regular basis?

9. Quarterly task lists for the minister and all staff members that are reviewed on a regular basis?

10. A system for congregants to have input into the minister's evaluation?

11. A process for the church council to evaluate the minister's performance at least annually?

Firing the Religious Leader

Does your church have:

12. Written procedures for firing the religious leader?

13. Procedures for congregational input before firing the religious leader?

14. An attorney to give the church council legal advice on procedures to follow when firing the religious leader?

The Church Council

Does your church have:

15. A written description of the role of the church council?

16. A written description of how council members are selected?

17. A notice of procedures to follow if a congregant is interested in being selected to serve on the council?

18. Written procedures of steps for a congregant to take to obtain permission to address the church council?

19. A list of the dates and times of all council meetings?

20. A system for obtaining the minutes of each council meeting?

Meaningful By-Laws

Does your church have:

21. Written by-laws?

22. A by-laws committee that reviews the by-laws in detail at least annually?

23. A system which makes it easy to change by-laws?

Forming Active Committees

Does your church have:

24. A list of all committees that is included in the church bulletin every few issues?

25. An available list of each committee with information about its responsibilities and how often it meets?

26. A folder that includes the minutes of each committee meeting?

Personnel Policies

Does your church have:

27. Written detailed personnel policies that cover the minister and all staff members?

28. A personnel committee that reviews the personnel policies at least annually?

Fiscal Procedures and Cutting Expenditures

Does your church have:

29. A balanced budget?

30. A budget that is available for review by all congregants?

31. A list of receipts, expenditures, and profits from all major events?

32. A finance committee that reviews the budget line-by-line at least once a year to see which receipts can be increased and which expenditures can be decreased?

33. A system of sending all congregants an annual list of all contributions they have made to the church with a designation of which contributions are tax-deductible?

Faith-Based Grant Writing

Does your church have:

34. A committee that reviews grant opportunities from government agencies, foundations, and businesses?

35. A staff member or volunteer with the ability and time to draft proposals for funding sources?

Effective Fundraising

Does your church have:

36. A fundraising committee that meets regularly to develop and implement a church fundraising plan?

37. A committee that meets to plan each fundraising event?

38. A system of recording the receipts and expenditures of each fundraising activity?

39. A system to record the time contributed by each volunteer?

Capital Campaigns

Does your church have:

40. A system for planning for long-term needs to expand the church or build a new one?

41. Procedures for contracting with a consultant to assist in capital campaigns?

Strategic Planning

Does your church have:

42. A current, detailed strategic plan that is updated at least once a year?

43. A system for getting congregational input into strategic planning?

44. A plan that has specific measurable objectives with a timetable for implementation?

45. A planning committee that meets at least quarterly to review the plan to see that it is being implemented effectively?

Membership and Programming

Does your church have:

46. A written description of the steps to take to join the church?

47. A system of contacting potential members and inviting them to join the church?

48. A list of various church programs and steps to take to participate in each program?

49. A listing of all church members on the computer with detailed demographics?

50. A system of contacting members and asking them for ideas for new programs in which they might be interested?

51. A system of meeting with "special interest groups" of church members (for example, teenagers, senior citizens, parents of young children) to explore the ways the church can meet their needs?

Getting and Keeping Volunteers

Does your church have:

52. A job description for every volunteer opportunity, including council membership, committees, office assistance, and special events?

53. A form for all congregants to fill out to apply for volunteer opportunities?

54. A system of interviewing congregants and assigning them to volunteer opportunities?

55. A system of keeping records of volunteer time so volunteers so can be thanked appropriately?

56. Numerous opportunities for thanking volunteers for their service to the church?

Meaningful Life-Cycle Events

Does your church have:

57. A written detailed instruction sheet for every major life-cycle event, such as birth, baptism, confirmation, conversion, marriage, and death?

Appendix 1: Hiring an Imam

From madisonmuslims.org

The Imam Hiring Committee (IHC) is assigned the task of searching for and selecting an imam for our community. It shall do it following guidelines listed herein within a reasonable time frame. Proper and standard hiring procedures shall also be upheld and consulted when needed.

The IHC shall:

1. Make all necessary steps so that its work is completed within three months of its first meeting.

2. Report directly to the Board of Masjid Us Sunnah.

3. Carry out tasks and obtain and exchange information about the candidates and all decisions about them in complete confidentiality.

4. Receive financial support from Masjid Us Sunnah to cover all related expenses and shall work within the limits of the budget specified for that. If needed, IHC may request increase of budget from the Masjid Us Sunnah Board. Compensation and benefit package for the selected candidate shall be determined and guaranteed by the Masjid Us Sunnah Board.

5. Draw a list of qualifications for the imam's position as well as the terms of agreement for it, including a set of key performance factors (KPF) for evaluation and development within the duration of the agreement.

6. Produce, and submit to the Masjid Us Sunnah Board, a scheduled plan of its objectives and tasks.

7. Maintain timely and effective communication, through its president, with the Masjid Us Sunnah Board.

8. Recognize that the final choice of a selected imam will be that of the Masjid Us Sunnah Board since the responsibilities associated with such decision lie with it.

Re: Fulltime Imam Position

Duties of the Imam:

- Lead the daily prayers at the Masjid.
- Deliver Jum'ah and Eid Khutbah except when there is a guest Khateeb.
- Give lectures for the Islamic education of the community on a weekly basis.
- Conduct regular Quran learning classes for children in the community.
- Lead the Taraweeh prayers during Ramadan.
- Should be available as a resource for educational, dawah, and youth programs.
- Provide matrimonial services as needed.
- Conduct funeral services and assist with body preparation and burial as needed.
- Provide counseling and guidance services as needed.

General Duties and Expectations:

- The Imam is expected to work about 40 hours a week, although additional time may be needed during Ramadan, Eid, and other special occasions.
- The Imam is expected to maintain regular and convenient office hours at the Masjid for members of the community to consult and seek guidance.
- The Imam shall interact with all persons and organizations, Muslim and non-Muslim.
- The Imam shall conduct himself at all times in ways that foster unity and a sense of inclusion among all

members of the local Muslim community and promote broad participation in community activities.

- The Imam shall not discriminate against any Muslim on the basis of Islamic school of jurisprudence, gender, race, national or ethnic origin, citizenship or immigration status, political affiliation, class, or economic status.

- The Imam shall adhere to the Bylaws of Masjid Us Sunnah and the policies set by its Boards and Executive Committee.

Salary and Benefits

Selected candidate will be offered a comprehensive salary and benefits package, which will include basic salary, paid vacation, and sick leave.

Appendix 2:
Advertisment for Imam

From ummah.com

Islamic Society in Alabama Seeks a Full-Time Imam

The Birmingham Islamic Society (BIS) is seeking a full-time Imam to lead its religious activities, give classes on Islamic matters, provide religious guidance, lead the Jummah salat, and participate in the youth and other programs. Birmingham has a diverse and rapidly growing Muslim community of more than 1,000 families and many college and K–12 students. The BIS's Masjids are located in spacious facilities in the cities of Hoover and Homewood, which are suburbs of the city of Birmingham. The community is seeking a dynamic leader with strong interpersonal skills and a vision for Islam in American society. Candidates must be well versed in Islamic Law (Shari'a), be fluent in English and classical Arabic, have a minimum of two years of experience as an Imam or assistant Imam in the West, and be eligible to work legally in the U.S. Excellent salary commensurate with experience. To apply, send a resume to....

Appendix 3:
United Church of Christ
Profile Reference

From ucc.org

You have received this reference form from a person who values your opinion. The material you provide will be placed with other materials to form a Ministerial Profile for use in the United Church of Christ. The Office for Parish, Life and Leadership encourages persons regularly to update or prepare a new profile. Therefore, being asked to provide a reference does not necessarily imply that the person is interested in a change in position. The material you provide may be used in the future by search committees if the person seeks a change. When the profile is completed, this information will be made available to the person about whom it is written.

When you have completed the information, please send this form with your signature directly to.... If you use a personal computer to prepare Section 2, we encourage you to provide a printed page and send this with your completed reference form. This will simplify the process of incorporating your comments into the person's Ministerial Profile. Profiles will not be distributed without references, so your prompt reply will be appreciated by the applicant.

You are being asked to provide as clear a picture of this person as possible through a forced choice checklist and commentary. Indicate the qualities evidenced in this person's ministry at this time as you have encountered them, both on the checklist and with at least a paragraph that will be compiled with other references to profile this person.

Reference for:

Name of Person Providing Reference (Rev., Dr., Mr., Ms.):

Signature of Person Providing Reference:

Address

City, State, ZIP

How Long and in What Relationship Have You Known the Above Named Person?

Section 1

This part of the reference form is for you to identify the 12 strongest qualities in this person's ministry as you have experienced it. There are no assumptions that items not marked are a sign of weakness in those areas. Check no more than 12. Many more characteristics will be apparent to you. Please indicate the strongest qualities from those on the second page of this form by placing an "X" beside them. Do not rank the 12. Because of the variety of items, read through them before beginning to mark items.

Fill out both sections. Return signed form to the address listed above.

Reference for: Date:

REFERENCES WILL NOT BE PROCESSED IF
MORE THAN 12 ITEMS ARE CHECKED.

___ 1.   is an effective preacher/speaker.

___ 2.   continues to develop his/her theological and Biblical skills.

___ 3.   helps people develop their spiritual life.

___ 4.   helps people work together in solving problems.

___ 5.   is effective in planning and leading worship.

___ 6.   has a sense of the direction of his/her ministry.

___ 7.   regularly encourages people to participate in United Church of Christ activities and programs.

___ 8. helps people understand and act upon issues of social justice.

___ 9. is a helpful counselor.

___ 10. ministers effectively to people in crisis situations.

___ 11. makes pastoral calls on people in hospitals and nursing homes and those confined to their homes.

___ 12. makes pastoral calls on members not confined at home or in hospitals.

___ 13. is a good leader.

___ 14. is effective in working with children.

___ 15. builds a sense of fellowship among the people with whom he/she works.

___ 16. helps people develop their leadership abilities.

___ 17. is an effective administrator.

___ 18. is effective with committees and officers.

___ 19. is an effective teacher.

___ 20. has a strong commitment to the educational ministry of the church.

___ 21. is effective in working with adults.

___ 22. inspires a sense of confidence.

___ 23. works regularly at bringing new members into the church.

___ 24. regularly encourages support of Our Church's Wider Mission.

___ 25. reaches out to inactive members.

___ 26. works regularly in the development of stewardship growth.

___ 27. is active in ecumenical relationships and encourages the church to participate.

___ 28. is a person of faith.

___ 29. writes clearly and well.

___ 30. works well on a team.

___ 31. is effective in working with youth.

___ 32. organizes people for community action.

___ 33. is skilled in planning and leading programs.

___ 34. plans and leads well-organized meetings.

___ 35. encourages people to relate their faith to their daily lives.

___ 36. is accepting of people with divergent backgrounds and traditions.

___ 37. encourages others to assume and carry out leadership.

___ 38. is mature and emotionally secure.

___ 39. has strong commitment and loyalty to the United Church of Christ.

___ 40. maintains confidentiality.

___ 41. understands and interprets the mission of the church from a global perspective.

___ 42. is a compassionate and caring person, sensitive to others' needs.

___ 43. deals effectively with conflict.

Section 2

Comment in a paragraph or two on personal qualities and characteristics that commend this person for ministry in the church (e.g., personal faith, adaptability to new ideas, integrity, etc.). Add anything you want to say that would be helpful. Please type or use a computer to write your comments on an additional page. If those are not available, please write legibly so that the comments may be accurately transcribed.

Appendix 4:
Pastoral Questionnaire

From The Alban Guide to Managing the Pastoral
Search Process *by John Vonhof (Alban Institute, 1999)*

Please write a few thoughts about each topic listed below. We
are interested, for your sake and ours, in relevant and concise statements of your thoughts and feelings as these phrases relate to you
and your ministry.

Personal Information:

Name: _____

Age: _____   Years Pastoring: _____

Home Phone: _____   Office Phone: _____

E-mail: _____

Fax: _____

Spiritual gifts:

1) _____

2) _____

3)_____

My most challenging ministry areas are:

My most satisfying ministry areas are:

My growth areas are:

Why do you want to change churches?

What is missing in your current church that you would like to find with us?

Spouse's Name: _____

Does your spouse have a role in your ministry or in the church?

If so, please describe.

Children:

1)_____ Age_____   2)_____ Age_____

3)_____ Age_____   4)_____ Age_____

5)_____ Age_____

Do you own your own home? Yes_____ No_____

Would you prefer to live in a parsonage _____
or your own home _____?

Your Thoughts About Leadership:

My style of leadership is:

My relationship to the board will be:

My relationship to staff and committee leaders will be:

Developing and nurturing a vision means:

Involving others in lay ministry means:

I mentor others by:

I foster commitment and accountability by:

Your Thoughts About Administration

Administration of the church should be:

The board and committees assist in church's administration by:

Your Thoughts About Worship:

The worship style I prefer is:

My preaching and teaching styles are:

Lay participation should include:

I think formal and informal worship are:

Your Thoughts About Education:

Good children and youth programs include:

Family ministry means:

Adult education should be:

Your Thoughts About Evangelism:
Evangelism allows the church to:

Training others for evangelism means:

Evangelism should be:

Your Thoughts About Fellowship:
Good church fellowship is:

I think family visiting is:

Caring for each other means:

Questions you might have for us? Please write any questions you may have on another piece of paper.

Appendix 5:
Model for Congregational Stewardship

With permission of Pastor Richard L. Dowhower of Mechanicsburg, PA

This proposal is based upon the following *understandings:*

1. Christian stewardship is how a person of faith manages the gifts of person, abilities, resources and opportunities which one believes God has provided. Christian stewardship is broader in scope than simply what one does at, for and with the church.

2. A mature Christian steward is most likely to pledge time, effort and money when asked face-to-face to do so by a fellow Christian known and respected who holds up *an inspired vision* for congregational and global ministry that connects with the steward's faith commitments for mission.

3. A mature Christian steward actually gets *personally excited* at the prospects of serving, committing and giving away one's resources as a confirming witness to one's faith.

A Traditional Model of a
Year-Long Stewardship Program

Month	Activity	Assignment
February	Recruit Stewardship Committee	Council
March	Design campaign & assign duties	Stewardship Committee - Begin two months of stewardship education
April	Plan and announce 2012 mission envisioning by all committees and organizations asking "What would you really like to do next year?" "What is God calling us to do?"	Stewardship
May	Visit each committee /organization to check on and assist progress in envisioning	Stewardship and Committees
June	Compile proposed goals for next year	Council
July	Cost out (time, talent, money) proposed goals. Prepare pledge cards for time, talent, treasure	Finance Committee Stewardship
August	Plan & recruit for every member visit by (1) home visits, or (2) neighborhood meetings, or (3) special banquet event	Stewardship
September	Approve 2012 Proposal and announce theme	Council
October	Take proposal to members and friends at face-to-face event chosen above: objective is returned & signed pledge cards on Consecration Sunday	Stewardship, recruits and council
November	2012 budget built, based on proposal & pledging evaluation of campaign	Finance, Council Stewardship
December	2012 budget presented for approval	Congregational Meeting

Each monthly step of such a campaign would require the following:

(1) A feature article in THE MESSENGER

(2) A Temple Talk

(3) Bulletin announcements and inserts twice monthly

(4) An email news article twice monthly

Additional resources to be deployed:

(1) Pastoral preaching and teaching

(2) Personal testimonials from respected mature steward members

(3) Guest speakers

(4) Appeal to alumni and other friends of the congregation

Appendix 6:
Sample Registration Card

From High Expectations: The Remarkable Secret for Keeping People in Your Church *by Thom S. Rainer (Boardman & Holman, 1999)*

Welcome to _____

Date _____

Dr./Rev./Ms./Mr./Mrs./Miss _____

Phone _____

Address _____ Apt._____

Work Phone _____

City _____ State _____ Zip_____

Is This Your...

_____ First time? I came as a guest _____

_____ Second time? _____ Third time? _____ Attender _____ Member

Present Church Membership _____

Your School Grade	or Age Group	Please Circle:
K 1 2 3 4 5 6 7 8	18–29 30–35 36–40 41–45	Single
9 10 11 12 College	46–49 50–55 56–64 65–66+	Married

Names of your children living at home: Birthday:

_____

_____

_____

I'd like information on: I would like to:

__ How to become a Christian   __ Commit my life to Christ

__ Next membership class   __ Renew my commitment to Christ

__ Spiritual growth   __ Be baptized

__ Teacher training   __ Be enrolled in next membership class

__ Missions   __ Help where needed

__ Adult Bible study   __ Enroll in Sunday School

__ Music activities   __ Join the church

__ Singles activities   __ Reservations for Wed. night dinner

__ College activities

__ Youth activities

__ Preschool children activities

Would you like a prayergram sent to the person prayed for?

_____

Appendix 7:
Membership Application

From Pine Street Presbyterian Church, Harrisburg, PA.

We are pleased to know that you are responding to Christ's call to unite with this church. Please read through and complete this application in preparation for meeting together informally with several elders from the Session (the church governing body).

Date:_____

Mr., Mrs., Miss, Ms., Dr. (please circle as appropriate)

Your name (as you would like it to appear in church publications):

_____

Your full name for record purposes (married women please include birth family name):

_____

Home address, including city, state and zip code:

_____

_____

Home Phone: _____

Work Phone: _____

E-mail Address: _____

Cell Phone: _____

Requirements for Membership

The primary requirement for membership in the Presbyterian Church (USA) is a commitment to Jesus Christ as Lord and Savior and a willingness to live out this commitment daily in your life as an active member of a local church.

You may unite with Pine Street Presbyterian Church in one of several ways. Please check the one most appropriate for you.

___ I profess faith in Jesus Christ as Lord and Savior, and request to be baptized.

___ I was baptized as a child but this will be the first time I have publically professed that faith and united with a local church.

___ Though a member of another Christian Church, I have been inactive for some time, and would like to unite with Pine Street by reaffirming my baptismal commitments to Jesus Christ as Lord and Savior.

___ I am currently a member of another Christian church and wish to transfer that membership to Pine Street Church as an active member. Please write for a letter of transfer at:

Church Name   Pastor's Name

_____

Church Address, if known, including city, state, and zip code

_____

I am an active member of _____ and plan to return to that church when I complete my time of work/study/service in Harrisburg. I would like to retain that membership and become an Affiliate member of Pine Street Presbyterian Church.

Membership at Pine Street is both exciting and demanding. The Session at Pine Street asks prospective members to attempt to meet the following membership standards:

- Weekly attendance at worship

- Commitment to personal prayer and bible reading on a daily basis

- Financial support through an annual pledge to Pine Street Church, using the biblical guide of a tithe (10% of one's income), or the promise to work toward this biblical standard while a member of this congregation

- The desire to share your faith with others as God provides appropriate opportunities

- Commitment to invite at least two non-churched friends to attend worship with you at Pine Street each year

- Willingness to assume any calling in the life of the church as your gifts, talents and family/work responsibilities allow

Date of Birth: _____ / _____ / _____

Place of Birth (city and state):_____

Marital status: (please check appropriate category)

___ single ___ engaged ___ married (date)_____/_____/_____

___ widowed ___ separated ___ divorced

Occupation: _____

Business Address: _____

City, State, Zip Code: _____

Phone Number: _____

Family Members: _____

Spouse: _____

Date of Birth: _____/_____/_____ Member: _____ yes _____ no

Child(ren): ___

Date of Birth: _____/_____/_____ Member: _____ yes _____ no

Grade in school if applicable

Child(ren): ___

Date of Birth: _____/_____/_____ Member: _____ yes _____ no

Grade in school if applicable: ___

Child(ren): ___

Date of Birth: _____/_____/_____ Member: _____ yes _____ no

Grade in school if applicable: ___

Parents (if still living)

Names: _____

Address: _____

City, State and Zip Code: _____

Phone Number: _____

If you served as an Elder or Deacon in your previous church(es), please fill out the following: _____

Date and church where ordained: _____

Dates and other churches where you may have served as an Elder or Deacon: _____

Any other pertinent information you may have: _____

_____

_____

Appendix 8:
Topics Included in the
New Member Class

From High Expectations: The Remarkable Secret for Helping People in Your Church *by Thom S. Rainer (Broadman & Holman, 1999)*

1. Doctrine of the church.
2. Polity/government of church.
3. Examination of church constitution.
4. Purpose of the Lord's Supper/Communion and baptism.
5. Examination of church covenant/church discipline.
6. Policies of church discipline/exclusion of members.
7. Expectations of members after joining.
8. History of church.
9. Tour of church facilities.
10. Denominational information.
11. Plan of salvation.
12. Tithing/financial support of the church.
13. Method/meaning of baptism.
14. Requirements of membership.
15. Current opportunities for service in the church.
16. Training in spiritual disciplines.
17. Introduction to church staff and leadership.
18. Explanation of the church's mission and/or vision.
19. Inventory of spiritual gifts.

20. Structure/support of missions.
21. Training for witnessing/evangelism.

Appendix 9:
Questions to Ask

From A Parishioner's Guide to Understanding Parish Finance, *National Leadership Roundtable on Church Management, theleadershiproundtable.org.*

1. Does my parish have a finance council?
2. Does my parish finance council meet regularly and are the members' professional backgrounds appropriate for service on the finance council?
3. Does my parish/parish finance council publish the annual budget and are parish officials available to discuss the budget?
4. Does my parish routinely publish statistics including: number of registered parishioners, collection levels, school enrollment, along with an annual comprehensive financial statement which includes revenue, expenses, and a balance sheet?
5. Does my parish include statistics from prior years for comparison and identify trends?
6. Does my parish release quarterly or semi-annual "budget updates" which show actual revenues and expenses in comparison to the approved budget?
7. Does my parish have a rainy day or capital savings account?
8. Does my parish have policies on conflicts of interest, protection of whistleblowers as recommended by the United States Conference of Catholic Bishops Accounting Practices Committee?

9. Is there a regularly scheduled audit of the parish which is conducted by an independent outside auditor? Are the results of this audit made available to the parishioners?

10. Is there an annual diocesan/parish questionnaire which assesses the parish's financial controls and health? Is this document reviewed by the parish finance council and acted upon?

11. Are parish buildings inspected by a competent building inspector periodically for routine maintenance? Are the inspection results taken into account when budgeting?

12. Does my parish follow diocesan guidelines for handling offertory collections, such rotating teams of collection counters?

13. Are there oversight policies for receipt/handling and disbursement of parish funds handled by individuals?

14. Are bank and other account statements received and reviewed independently by more than one individual?

15. Are the individuals handling financial responsibilities in my parish cross trained so that if one becomes incapacitated another may perform that function?

Appendix 10:
Chart of Accounts

From Business Management in the Local Church *by David R. Pollock (Moody Press, 1992).*

Receipts

General Fund

301	Envelope Offerings
302	Loose Offerings
308	Interest on Savings Accounts
309	Miscellaneous Income

Mission Fund

321	Envelope Offerings
322	Special Offerings
329	Miscellaneous Income

Building Fund

341	Envelope Offerings
342	Special Offerings
349	Miscellaneous Income

Special Funds

361	Offerings
362	Special Gifts
363	Memorial Gifts
369	Miscellaneous Income

Disbursements

<u>General Fund</u>

Physical Plant

401   Heat

402   Utilities

403   Custodian Salaries

404   Social Security Tax

405   Janitorial Supplies

406   Insurance

407   Repair and Maintenance—Building and Grounds

408   Repair and Maintenance—Equipment

409   Telephone

410   Equipment

411   Bus Expense

412   Miscellaneous

Pastoral Ministry

421   Salary

422   Literature and Printing

423   Office Supplies

424   Pulpit Supply

425   Special Meetings Expense

426   Parsonage—Insurance

427   Pension Plan

428   Special Travel Allowances

429   Auto Allowance

430   Parsonage Utilities

Christian Education

441   Salary

442   Literature and Printing

443	Office Supplies
444	Pension Plan
445	Special Travel Allowances
446	Auto Allowance
447	Utilities Allowance

Worship Service

461	Music and Choir Expense
462	Literature and Printing
463	Office Supplies
464	Flowers

Miscellaneous General Expense

481	Special Gifts
482	Advertising
483	Office Salaries
484	Social Security Tax
485	Flowers
486	Miscellaneous

Mission Fund

| 501 | North American Baptist General Conference |
| 502 | (an account would be established and assigned an account number for each organization or person for which mission support is budgeted) |

Building Fund

601	Construction Projects
602	(an account would be established and assigned an account number for each project)
621	Interest Expense
622	Principal Payments

Special Funds

701   Library Fund, etc. (a separate account would be established for each fund which will not liquidate itself immediately)

721   Special Offerings

722   Special Gifts

723   Memorial Gifts

Appendix 11:
Sample Volunteer
Job Description

From Attracting and Managing Volunteers, A Parish Handbook *by Donna Pinsoneault (Ligouri Publications, 2001)*

Please adapt this format to suit the needs of people in your parish.

Job/Project name: _____

Summary of work: _____

When: _____

Where: _____

By Whom? _____

With Whom? _____

Accountable to: _____

The work is important to the parish because:

_____

_____

What qualifications will make the work easier?

_____

_____

What learning opportunities go along with taking this position?

_____

_____

What training is required?

_____

_____

What resources are available to support this work? (for example: financial, other volunteers, staff involvement, and so on)

_____

_____

Primary contact for answers to questions, help with solving problems, and so on:

_____

_____

Personal expenditures up to _____ will be reimbursed by _____.

Advance approval required for additional expenditures.

Required meetings: _____

Required written reports: _____

Term of service: _____

(Add any other information that volunteers will need to know to complete this work effectively.)

Appendix 12:
Talent Bank Questionnaire

From Pine Street Presbyterian Church, Harrisburg, PA.

Pine Street Church encourages members to be stewards of time as well as money. The ministries of our church depend on the efforts of all of our members. This questionnaire will help church leaders learn about your talents and interests and also help them match skills with needs. It is our hope that each of us can find ways to use our spiritual gifts and talents in ministry, regardless of our schedules or ages. Naturally, your acceptance of any request for your talents is contingent on your availability.

Please check any of the entries below which apply to you. If this is something you really like to do, place a "P" (preference) in place of a checkmark.

Name: (please print) _____

Telephone Number: _____

E-mail Address: _____

<u>DRIVING</u>: I can…

_____ drive someone to church on Sunday

_____ drive someone to church during the week:

_____daytime only _____evening only

_____ drive children and youth to activities and special events

_____ help provide transportation for special day trips

_____ provide the use of a truck for hauling

OFFICE HELP: I can…

_____ answer phones

(days and times available: _____)

_____ help organize church history records (Archives)

FOOD: I can…

_____ help prepare meals at church

_____ help with the Bread Baking Ministry

_____ bake items at home for fellowship activities

_____ help serve meals at church functions

_____ help to set up or clean up for church meals

_____ serve meals at Downtown Daily Bread

HEALTH CARE: I can…

_____ supply health care for those in need (specialties: _____)

_____ consult on health care concerns (specialties: _____)

_____ help coordinate access and information for health care needs

_____ offer in-home assistance to home bound members

TEACHING: I can…

_____ teach on special topics (identify topics: _____)

_____ serve as teacher or substitute for: _____ adult classes

_____ youth classes _____ children's classes

_____ help in church nursery

_____ serve as a fellowship advisor for youth groups

_____ chaperone fellowship events or oversight youth retreats

_____ help with bible study

_____ lead prayer fellowship

LABOR: I can…

_____ move furniture

_____ install furnishings (shelves, draperies, pictures)

_____ provide light housekeeping for the homebound members

_____ decorate the church for holiday events

_____ do lawn work spring/fall for homebound members

MUSIC: I can…

_____ sing with the choir

_____ play in the handbell choir

_____ play an instrument (please specify:_____)

_____ teach songs to children in Sunday School

_____ help organize special music presentations for the church

_____ play the piano for Church School Classes

ART/DRAMA: I can…

_____ help with adult crafts

_____ help with children's crafts

_____ help organize special art exhibits for the church

_____ help with costumes and make-up for plays, skits, etc.

_____ help with set design and stage craft

LIBRARY: I can…

_____ help sort and organize books

_____ do inventory

_____ follow-up on books which have been checked out

HOSPITALITY: I can…

_____ host social events

_____ visit homebound members

_____ host a church visitor (missionary, visiting speaker, etc.)

TECHNICAL: I can…

_____ set up and run PowerPoint equipment

_____ run the visual/audio system in the sanctuary

_____ help with the church's Website

OTHER: I can…

_____ assist with worship (e.g. scripture reading)

_____ participate on a committee (please specify: _____)

_____ participate in local mission projects

_____ share hobbies with others (please specify: _____)

_____ share job skills with others (please specify: _____)

_____ communion preparation and clean up

_____ count offering money

Appendix 13:
Ways to Support and Recognize Volunteers

From How to Mobilize Church Volunteers *by Marlene Wilson (Augsburg Publishing House, 1983).*

Volunteers in churches often are taken for granted. They, and the services they provide, often are unrecognized, unthanked, and unsupported. Yet, they deserve our recognition and gratitude. The role of the volunteer in the life and ministry of the church is an important one. Indeed, the life and ministry of the church depend on those who volunteer their time and effort to do the various tasks and services necessary or helpful for the effective and faithful functioning of the church. Without such volunteers there probably would be no church or ministry or society as we know them today.

Following is a beginning list of ways to support and recognize volunteers and the work they do within the local church, in the wider church, and in the community. Add your own creative ideas and then plan how to implement as many as possible.

- Publish a list of persons who volunteer within the local church, in the wider church, and in the community and distribute it to the church members, post it on bulletin boards, or carry it in the church newsletter.

- Plan a worship service around the theme of volunteer ministry.

- Plan a volunteer recognition dinner, invite all volunteers, and honor them with speeches, skits, certificates, awards, gifts.

- Reimburse the out-of-pocket costs volunteers incur as part of their volunteer ministries.

- Ask for a report.

- Send a birthday, anniversary, or Christmas card.

- Provide child care service to enable mothers and fathers of young children to volunteer.

- Keep challenging volunteers.

- Provide good orientation, on-the-ministry training, and continuing education opportunities.

- Provide occasions for volunteers to get together for informal sharing of their experiences.

- Give additional responsibility.

- Send newsworthy information about the work of volunteers to the local newspapers.

- Have a party for volunteers.

- Create pleasant surroundings for their work and meetings.

- Take time to talk with volunteers and express appreciation for their efforts.

- Share the positive comments you hear about volunteers and their work with them.

- Provide scholarships and expense money for volunteers to attend training and continuing education workshops.

- Write them thank-you notes.

- Celebrate outstanding projects and achievements.

- Provide good resources and equipment for their use.

- Praise volunteers to their friends.

- Provide opportunities for individual conferences.

- Maintain an accurate record of their training and work and be prepared to provide a reference for the volunteers when they seek employment or other volunteer ministries.

- Plan a volunteer-of-the-month program or emphasis. For example: September—educational ministry workers; November—conference and association volunteers; January—official board; February—committee members; March—community volunteers; April—choir and music. Recognize these people in the church newsletter, the Sunday morning worship service, by placing their pictures on the church bulletin board.

- Send a letter of appreciation to the person's family.

- Honor groups and individuals in the groups.

- Have a picnic for volunteers.

- Say "Thank you!"

- Smile.

- Publicize information concerning recognition that members of the church have received for their volunteer work in other groups, institutions, or agencies.

- Ask volunteers to write statements on "Why I serve in the church" and publish them in the church newsletter.

- Give a gift of appreciation, for example, a certificate of recognition, a book, or other memento appropriate to their ministry.

- Provide opportunities for volunteers to assess their satisfactions, needs, learning, and growth in ministry.

- Form volunteer support groups for sharing joys and concerns.

- Provide opportunities for members to develop or create ministries to match and use their skills and interests.

Appendix 14:
Life-Cycle Forms

From Calvary Lutheran Church, Philadelphia, PA.

Wedding

Calvary Lutheran Church
5400 Springfield Avenue
Philadelphia, PA 19143
215-724-2311

Bride's Name _____

Address _____

City _____

State _____ ZIP _____

Telephone _____

Occupation _____

Age _____ Parents' Permission _____

Mother's Name _____

Father's Name _____

Groom's Name _____

Address _____

City _____

State _____ ZIP _____

Telephone _____

Occupation _____

Age _____ Parents' Permission _____

Mother's Name _____

Father's Name _____

Wedding Date _____
Rehearsal Date _____

Place _____
Time _____
Bridal Party

Maid/Matron of Honor _____

Flower Girl _____

Attendants _____

Groom's Party

BestMan _____

Ring Bearer _____

Ushers _____

Organist _____

Assisting Minister _____

Soloist _____

Florist _____

Acolyte _____

Photographer _____

Sexton _____

Church Fee _____

Reception _____

License Received _____

Certificate Issued _____

License Returned _____

Funeral

Name _____

Address _____

City _____

State _____ ZIP _____

Date of Birth _____

Date of Death _____

Date of Funeral _____

Place of Funeral _____

Time _____

Funeral Home _____

Family Contact _____

Address _____

Telephone _____

Pall Bearers _____

Church Records Updated _____

Spouse _____

Children _____

Siblings _____

Other Relatives _____

Special Requests _____

Favorite Scripture Passages _____

Favorite Hymns _____

Notes

Introduction

1. Hartford Institute for Religion Research, "Fast Facts About American Religion," *http://hirr.hartsem.edu/research/fastfacts/fast_facts.html.*

2. Ibid.

3. ProCon.Org, *http://undergod.procon.org/view.resource.php?resourceID=000068.*

4. Ibid.

5. The Pew Forum on Religion & Public Life, a project of the Pew Research Center, a subsidiary of the Pew Charitable Trusts, 2010, *http://religions.pewforum.org/pdf/report2religious-landscape-study-key-findings.pdf.*

6. Thesaurus.com. *www.thesaurus.com.*

Chapter 1: Hiring the Religious Leader

1. Code of Canon Law: Section 523, *www.vatican.va/archive/ENG1104/_P1U.HTM.*

2. Jack M. Tuell, *The Organization of the United Methodist Church* (Nashville, Tenn.: Abingdon Press, 1973), 45–46.

3. Hiring an Imam, *www.madisonmuslims.org.*

4. Office of Vocation, Presbyterian Church (USA), *Committee On Ministry Advisory Handbook* (2008).

5. The Search and Call Process in the United Church of Christ, *www.ucc.org/ministers/search-and-call/section-3-the-search-and-call-process-in-the-ucc.pdf*, 3.

6. Ibid.

7. John Vonhof, *The Alban Guide to Managing the Pastoral Search Process* (Herndon, Va.: Alban Institute, 1999), 2–3.

8. The Search and Call Process in the United Church of Christ, 9–10.

9. Rabbi Elliot Schoenberg, "The Rabbinic Search as an Uplifting Religious Experience" (The Rabbinic Assembly, 2008), 3.

10. The Presbyterian Church (USA), *On Calling a Pastor: A Manual for Churches Seeking Pastors: Revised Edition*, (2007), 23.

11. Vonhof, 61.

12. Vonhof, 33.

13. The Search and Call Process in the United Church of Christ, 9–10.

14. *On Calling a Pastor.* The Presbyterian Church (USA), 27.

15. The Search and Call Process in the United Church of Christ, 17.

16. Baptists: Two Church Officers: Pastors and Deacons, *www.baptistdistinctives.org/articles/twochurchofficers.shtml*.

17. By-laws—Unitarian Universalist Church of Harrisburg, Pa.

18. Mormon Religion, *www.mormon.org*.

19. *The Baha'i Faith.* US Baha'is Distribution Service: Atlanta.

20. New World Encyclopedia, "Wicca," *www.newworldencyclopedia.org/entry/Wicca*.

Chapter 2: Supporting the Religious Leader

1. William G. Caldwell, "Personnel Administration" in *Church Administration Handbook*, Bruce P. Powers (ed.) (Nashville, Tenn.: B&H Publishing Group, 2008), 99–100.

Chapter 3: Evaluating the Religious Leader and Staff

1. Office of Vocation, Presbyterian Church (USA), *Committee On Ministry Advisory Handbook* (2008).

2. Ibid.

3. Jill M. Hudson, *When Better Isn't Enough: Evaluation Tools for the 21st Century Church* (Herndon, Va.: Alban Institute, 2004), 104–117.

4. David R. Pollock, *Business Management in the Local Church* (Chicago: Moody Press, 1992), 216.

5. Ibid., 216–217.

6. George H. Hunter, III, *Leading and Managing a Growing Church* (Nashville, Tenn.: Abingdon Press, 2000), 99–100.

Chapter 4: Firing the Religious Leader

1. By-laws—Unitarian Universalist Church of Harrisburg, Pa.

2. Baptists: Two Church Officers: Pastors and Deacons, *www.baptistdistinctives.org/articles/ twochurchofficers.shtml*

3. United Synagogue of Conservative Judaism. "The USCJ Guide to Contractual Relations," 3.

4. Ibid., 11

5. William G. Caldwell, "Personnel Administration" in *Church Administration Handbook*, Bruce P. Powers (ed.) (Nashville, Tenn.: B&H Publishing Group, 2008), 110.

Chapter 5: The Council

1. *One Who Serves, Parish Pastoral Council Norms and Guidelines* (Diocese of Harrisburg, Pa.,2005), 4.

2. Bruce P. Powers, "Organizing for Mission and Ministry" in *Church Administration Handbook,* Bruce P. Powers (ed.) (Nashville, Tenn.: B&H Publishing Group, 2008), 41.

3. Dan Hotchkiss, *Governance and Ministry* (Herndon, Va.: Alban Institute 2009), 114.

4. Norman Shawchuck and Roger Hueser, *Managing the Congregation* (Nashville: Abingdon Press, 1996), 114.

5. Michael A. Sand, *How to Manage an Effective Nonprofit Organization* (Franklin Lakes, N.J.: Career Press, 2005), 50–51.

6. Hotchkiss, 119.

7. Larry Osborne, *Sticky Teams* (Grand Rapids, Mich.: Zondervan, 2010), 35.

8. Ibid., 37.

9. Ibid., 101–102.

10. Ibid., 112.

11. *Book of Order, The Constitution of the Presbyterian Church (USA) Part II, 2007–2009)* Section W-1.4005.

12. Ibid., Section W-l.4004 (e)(f).

13. Hotchkiss, 64.

14. Osborne, 140.

15. Baptist Congregational Church Governance: A Challenge *www.baptistdistinctives.org/articles/congregationalchurchgovernancechallenge.shtml.*

16. Ibid.

17. Robert D. Dale, "Working With People: The Minister as Team Leader" in *Church Administration Handbook,* Bruce P. Powers (ed.) (Nashville, Tenn.: B&H Publishing Group, 2008), 83–84.

18. R.W.P. Patterson, "A Practical *How To* Guide For Church Board Members," *www.HospitalityPlus.org.*

19. Ibid., 7.

20. Ibid., 8.

Chapter 6 Meaningful By-Laws

1. Larry Osborne, *Sticky Teams* (Grand Rapids, Mich.: Zondervan), 44.

2. Donald Kramer, "Nonprofit Issues" Ready Reference (June 16–30, 2005), 82.

3. Ibid.

4. Osborne, 43.

Chapter 9: Effective Fundraising

1. Kim Klein, *Ask and You Shall Receive: Leader Manual* (San Francisco, Calif.: Jossey-Bass, 2000), 2.

2. Wendy Cadge and Robert Wuthnow, "Religion and the Nonprofit Sector" in *The Nonprofit Sector* (New Haven: Yale University Press, Conn. 2006), 498.

3. Lyle E. Schaller, *44 Questions for Congregational Self-Appraisal* (Nashville, Tenn.: Abingdon Press), 121–125.

Chapter 12: Faith-Based Grant Writing

1. Joy Skjegstad, *Winning Grants to Strengthen Your Ministry* (Herndon, Va.: Alban Institute, 2007), 45–47.

2. Ibid, 46.

3. Ibid.

4. Joy Skjegstad, *Starting a Nonprofit at Your Church* (Herndon, Va.: Alban Institute, 2002), 4–9.

5. Joy Skjegstad, *Winning Grants to Strengthen Your Ministry* (Herndon, Va.: Alban Institute, 2007), 31.

6. White House Office of the Press Secretary, February 5, 2009.

7. Frequently Asked Questions (FAQs) about the Center for Faith-Based and Neighborhood Partnerships, *www.commerce.gov*.

8. Ibid.

9. Ibid.

Chapter 13: Strategic Planning

1. Alvin Lindgren, *Foundations for Purposeful Church Administration*, (New York: Abingdon Press, 1965), 226.

2. Ibid.

3. Cultivating the Future: Long-Range Planning for Congregations (Union for Reform Judaism, 2006), 4.

4. Lindgren, 236.

Chapter 14: Membership and Programming

1. Rick Warren, *The Purpose Driven Church* (Grand Rapids, Mich.: Zondervan, 1995), 257–263.

2. "Welcome to Holy Spirit Catholic Church," Palmyra, Pa.

3. Jack M. Tuell, *The Organization of The United Methodist Church* (Nashville, Tenn.: Abingdon Press, 1973), 47.

4. Thom S. Rainer, *High Expectations: The Remarkable Secret for Keeping People in Your Church* (Nashville, Tenn.: Broadman & Holman, 1999), 106.

5. Warren, 319.

6. Rainer, 24.

7. Ibid, 87.

8. Ibid, 89.

9. Larry Osborne, *Sticky Teams* (Grand Rapids, Mich.: Zondervan, 2010), 114.

Chapter 15: Getting and Keeping Volunteers

1. Wendy Cadge and Robert Wuthnow, "Religion and the Nonprofit Sector" in *The Nonprofit Sector* (New Haven, Conn.: Yale University Press, 2006), 498.

2. Marlene Wilson, *How to Mobilize Church Volunteers* (Minneapolis, Minn.: Augsburg Publishing House, 1983), 68.

3. Cadge and Wuthnow, 498.

Chapter 16: Meaningful Life-Cycle Events

1. Rev. Kenneth Koehler, *Preparing a Catholic Funeral* (Denver, Colo.: Living the Good News, 2004).

Recommended Reading

Administration in the Small Membership Church by John H. Tyson (Abingdon Press, 2007)

Ask and You Shall Receive: A Fundraising Training Program for Religious Organizations and Projects (Participant Manual and Leader Manual) by Kim Klein (Jossey-Bass, 2000)

Attracting and Managing Volunteers: A Parish Handbook by Donna Pinsoneault (Ligouri Publications, 2001)

Book of Order: The Constitution of the Presbyterian Church (USA) Part II (2007–2009) (Office of the General Assembly, Presbyterian Church, 2007)

Business Management in the Local Church by David R. Pollock (Moody Press, 1995)

The Catholic Fact Book by John Deedy (Tabor Publishing, 1986)

Church Administration Handbook edited by Bruce Powers (B&H Publishing Group, 2008)

The Church Administration Kit by Gene Grate (Beacon Hill Press, 2008)

The Church Treasurer's Manual: A Practical Guide for Managing Church Finances by Bruce Nuffer (Beacon Hill Press, 2008)

The Essential Nonprofit Fundraising Handbook: Getting the Money You Need from Government Agencies, Businesses, Foundations, and Individuals by Michael A. Sand and Linda Lysakowski (Career Press, 2009)

Excellent Catholic Parishes: The Guide to Best Places and Practices by Paul Wilkes (Paulist Press, 2001)

Foundations for Purposeful Church Administration by Alvin J. Lindgren (Abingdon Press, 1965)

Governance and Ministry: Rethinking Board Leadership by Dan Hotchkiss (The Alban Institute, 2009)

High Expectations: The Remarkable Secret for Keeping People in Your Church by Thom S. Rainer (Broadman & Holman, 1999)

Holy Clarity: The Practice of Planning and Evaluation by Sarah Drummond (The Alban Institute, 2009)

How to Manage an Effective Nonprofit Organization by Michael A. Sand (Career Press, 2005)

How to Mobilize Church Volunteers by Marlene Wilson (Augsburg Publishing House, 1983)

Leading and Managing a Growing Church by George G. Hunter III (Abingdon Press, 2000)

Managing the Congregation: Building Effective Systems to Serve People by Norman Shawchuck and Roger Heuser (Abingdon Press, 1996)

Ministry and Management: The Study of Ecclesiastical Administration by Peter F. Rudge (Tavistock Publications, 1968)

The Nonprofit Sector: A Research Handbook edited by Walter W. Powell and Richard Steinberg (Yale University Press, 2006)

Pastoral Search: The Alban Guide to Managing the Pastoral Search Process by John Vonhof (The Alban Institute, 1999)

The Purpose Driven Church: Growth Without Compromising Your Message and Mission by Rick Warren (Zondervan, 1995)

The Organization of the United Methodist Church by Jack M. Tuell (Abingdon Press, 1973)

Starting a Nonprofit at Your Church by Joy Skjegstad (The Alban Institute, 2002)

Sticky Teams by Larry Osborne (Zondervan, 2010)

Strategic Leadership for a Change: Facing Our Losses, Finding Our Future by Kenneth J. McFayden (The Alban Institute, 2009)

Tempting Faith: An Inside Story of Political Seduction by David Kuo (Free Press, 2006)

Visions of Development: Faith-Based Initiatives by Wendy Tyndale (Ashgate Publishing, 2006)

The Volunteer Book: A Guide for Churches and Nonprofits by Denise Locker (Beacon Hill Press, 2010)

When Better Isn't Enough: Evaluation Tools for the 21st-Century Church by Jill M. Hudson (The Alban Institute, 2004)

Winning Grants to Strengthen Your Ministry by Joy Skjegstad (The Alban Institute, 2007)

Index

About the Author

Michael A. Sand is one of the country's leading experts in nonprofit management. He founded Sand Associates in 1982. It is a nationwide comprehensive management consulting firm based in Harrisburg, Pennsylvania, which specializes in helping nonprofit groups including religious organizations, government agencies, social service agencies, and arts groups. He received his bachelor's and doctor of laws degrees from the University of Pennsylvania and a master's degree in public administration from Penn State University. He has led more than 1000 workshops on topics such as grant writing, strategic planning, fundraising, and board development.

Michael A. Sand is the author of *How to Manage an Effective Nonprofit Organization* and *The Essential Nonprofit Fundraising Handbook*, both published by Career Press.

Contact information:

www.sandassociates.com

msand9999@aol.com